Notetaking & study skills

GLORIA HANSEN WEBER
Consultant
Forkner Publishing Corporation

HAMDEN L. FORKNER, JR.
Consultant
Forkner Publishing Corporation

EDWIN J. WEBER
Assistant Chairman
Department of Secondary and Adult Teacher Education
The University of New Mexico

FORKNER PUBLISHING CORPORATION
Ridgewood, New Jersey
A Subsidiary of Gage Publishing Limited

NOTETAKING AND STUDY SKILLS

Third Printing, 1980

3 4 5 6 7 8 9 0 F 3 2 1 0

Published by: Forkner Publishing Corporation, P.O. Box 652, Ridgewood, NJ 07451

Standard Book Number: 912036-27-3

Foreword

The transition from secondary school to college or university is difficult for most students. The year-by-year figures on the attrition of first-year college students confirm this fact. Today's typical freshman must adjust to new social demands, begin making career decisions, and budget both time and money. Last, but not least, college makes academic demands for which many students are unprepared.

This new book and supporting materials are designed to help students cope with these academic demands. This program—

. . . provides instruction in procedures and techniques for making notes from lectures, reading, and observation.

. . . develops facility in recording ideas quickly and accurately, using a writing system that blends a few symbols with the conventional letters of the alphabet.

. . . suggests approaches and techniques for planning, outlining, writing, and proofreading term papers and research studies.

. . . reviews freshman "spelling demons" and common punctuation pitfalls.

. . . offers help in learning how to learn based on psychological principles.

Because the emphasis throughout the program is on independent study, self-checks are an integral part of the learning activities. These informal tests enable students to check their own progress and to assess their strengths and weaknesses.

Supporting materials include the items indicated below.

Notetaking and Study Skills Handbook. This is a combination workbook and reference manual. It provides a variety of self-checks and optional activities to encourage the development of study skills and notetaking competence. For example, informal reading tests help students judge their ability to read and comprehend college texts. The *Handbook* also serves as a resource for producing superior written work. Included are three practical guides for the college beginner—"A Writer's Guide to Footnotes and Bibliography," "A Writer's Guide to Punctuation and Style," and "A Writer's Guide to Format."

Notetaking and Study Skills Profile. This 100-item inventory serves as a pre-test. It gives students an indication of their proficiency in notetaking and study skills—skills they know they will need when they continue their education.

Notetaking and Study Skills Tape Library. This 6-cassette program gives students help in learning the writing shortcuts. Included are words and other materials from both the text and *Handbook.* The tapes provide about 15 minutes of dictation material correlated with each text chapter.

The shorthand plates in the program have been written by three writers—Mary S. Lore, John G. Diefenbaker Senior High, Calgary, Canada, Gloria H. Weber, and Hamden L. Forkner, Jr.

We express our warm thanks to the many teachers who shared their experiences and offered suggestions for this program. We also acknowledge our great debt to the late Hamden L. Forkner not only for inventing the writing shortcuts that are embodied in this program but also for inspiring us on many occasions.

G.H.W., H.L.F., Jr., and E.J.W.

Table of Contents

Chapter 1

INTRODUCTION

Taking notes is second nature to most of us. We reach automatically for pencil and paper to write a phone number we want to remember. We take down instructions–tomorrow's assignment. We record directions–how to get to Debbie's summer cottage. We make shopping lists. We jot down the points to be covered in a talk or the agenda for a sales conference. Ours is a notetaking culture. And yet, few people have mastered the art of notetaking.

NOTETAKING PRINCIPLES

In college, and later on the job, you will rely heavily on the notes you take. As an aid to remembering, studying, and learning, you will take notes as you study books, listen to lectures, participate in discussions, conduct and observe experiments, and participate in meetings and conferences. In all these situations, good notes are vital because you simply cannot remember all the important things you hear, read, and observe.

Learning to make good notes helps you to–

. . . focus your attention.
. . . sharpen your memory of significant facts and ideas.
. . . organize what you hear, read, and observe.
. . . become a better writer.

Focusing your attention. Taking notes forces you to listen, read, and observe more effectively. You gear your mind to the speaker's or writer's train of thought, and your mind wanders less frequently. This book will help you to become an *active* participant in the communication process. Here you will find practical suggestions for listening and reading more attentively, for grasping the important points, and for recording them efficiently.

Sharpening your memory. Psychologists have shown that we forget much of the detail of what we learn within a few hours after we have learned it. But notetaking can help you minimize that forgetting. The process of taking notes helps you to fix main ideas in your mind–ideas that jog your memory and enable you to recall related facts and relationships.

We also know from psychological studies that you can relearn something you have forgotten much faster than you can learn that same thing for the first time. Obviously, notes are essential for this *relearning,* or *reviewing*, process. In this book you will find memory-jogging suggestions and aids to reviewing that will help you in school, college, and later in your business or professional life.

Organizing what you hear, read, and observe. Notemaking is more than just taking things down on paper. If your notes are to be useful in reviewing and studying, you need to know how to outline as you listen, how to make reading notes. This program will give you practical help in both what and how to record what you read and hear.

Becoming a better writer. Do you have difficulty planning and writing term papers, reports, and essay exams? If so, you are not alone because there are very few "natural" writers. Most of us need guidance and plenty of practice to learn to write clearly. After all, even professional writers need editors!

This program will help you to prepare outlines, do library research, and make reading notes. You will also benefit from examining and analyzing the errors most frequently made by college freshmen in their written work.

NOTETAKING MATERIALS

Plan to use a ball-point pen with a fine point to take notes and to practice your notetaking. If your instructor does not provide paper, buy a lined 21.6 by 26.9 cm. (8½" by 11") notebook or notebook paper with lines. If your normal handwriting is large, you should use "wide ruled" paper. If your handwriting is small, you can use paper with less space between the lines, known as "college ruled" paper.

When you take notes, leave a margin of at least 8 cm. (3") on the left side of each sheet. The shorter writing line permits you to write with more speed. Furthermore, the wide left margin comes in handy for adding marginal comments and questions when you review your notes. It is also a good idea to write on only one side of each sheet when taking notes. However, when you practice notetaking, write on both sides of each sheet in order to save paper.

TO CONSIDER AND DISCUSS

1. Name at least 3 ways in which good notes can help you?
2. What does it mean to be an "active" listener?
3. What do psychologists tell us about learning, forgetting, and relearning?

NOTETAKING APPLICATIONS

Your *Handbook* gives you self-checks to encourage you to apply the notetaking ideas and suggestions in the text. Because an answer key is provided with each self-check, you get immediate feedback on your performance. You may ask, "If the answers are there, why not simply copy them." You should not copy the key because then you will lose the benefits of feedback—an essential element in learning.

Now turn to Unit 1 in your *Handbook* and complete the "Notetaking and Study Skills Profile." Check your answers with the key and figure your profile score according to the instructions.

Chapter 2

BUILDING YOUR WRITING SPEED

To take good notes, you must be able to write fast. Of course, making good notes requires other skills too—ability to listen carefully, ability to figure out the speaker's or writer's organization of ideas, and the like. But ability to record thoughts quickly and accurately is essential.

HOW FAST CAN YOU WRITE?

Chances are, you have no idea how fast you can write longhand. Here is a test of writing speed that will give you your longhand writing rate in words a minute. Copy the sentence below on a separate piece of paper.

Jane will read each page with care.

Now, while someone times you (or you time yourself), copy the sentence as many times as you can in longhand for 15 seconds (one fourth of a minute). Write continuously until the 15 seconds are up.

To figure your writing speed in words a minute, count the total number of words you wrote in 15 seconds and multiply that figure by 4. For example, if you wrote the speed sentence once and finished the word, "read," the second time through, you wrote 10 words in one-fourth of a minute. Your longhand writing rate would be 40 words a minute (10 words x 4).

If you wrote less than 25 words a minute, you should practice writing longhand to build your speed. An average speed range is between 25 to 35 words a minute. If you wrote 35 to 45 words a minute, your speed is above that of most people. If you wrote over 45 words a minute, Congratulations! Only a few people write longhand this fast.

WRITING SHORTCUTS

An easy way to increase your notetaking speed is to leave out writing strokes you don't need. Look at a sample of your own writing. What do you see? Extra strokes, loops, and curls that slow down your writing? When you are taking notes or writing rough drafts of papers, begin now to eliminate every unnecessary writing stroke.

Omitting strokes on letters that begin words. The samples below show how to eliminate unneeded strokes on letters that come first in a word. Quickly write a line of each of these letters.

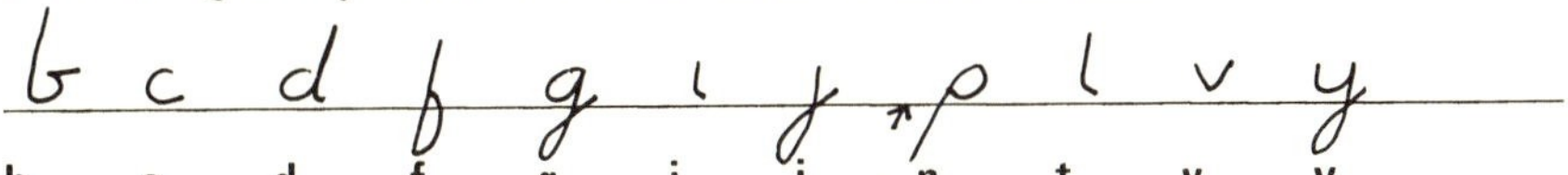

b c d f g i j p t v y

Learning tips. (1) To save time when you take notes, do not cross the *t* or dot the *i* or *j*. (2) When *p* begins a word, start below the line and make an upward stroke with a loop at the top.

Omitting strokes on letters that end words. Write each of the letters below several times, remembering to omit the extra ending strokes.

d f g j m n p r s y z

Writing by sound. You have seen how to save time by eliminating unneeded strokes in initial and final letters. Many writing strokes can also be saved if you write by sound. In notetaking, you write what you hear – and only what you hear. When you write by sound, you omit silent letters. The examples below show how to write by sound:

leave *lev* (You hear only *l*, *e*, and *v*.)

price *prus* (The *c* sounds like *s*, and the *e* is silent.)

easy *eze* (You hear only *e*, *z*, and *e*.)

edge *ej* (The *g* sounds like *j* and the *d* and final *e* are silent.)

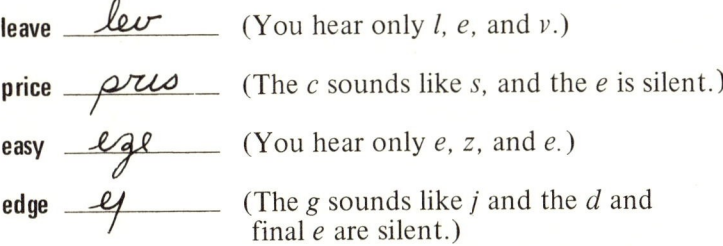

Cover the print and read the notetaking outlines below until you can read them as fast as you can read the print. Then cover the notetaking outlines, leaving the print visible. On a separate piece of paper, write the outlines from the print. Say each word to yourself as you write it. Better still, get someone to read the words to you (about one a second) while you write them. Practice writing the outlines until you can write one each second. Try to make your outlines look the same as those in the text. Remember, do not dot the *i* or *j* or cross the *t*.

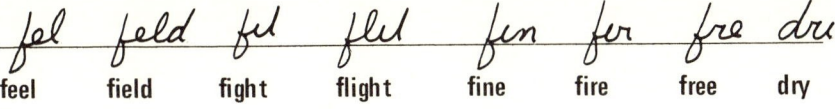

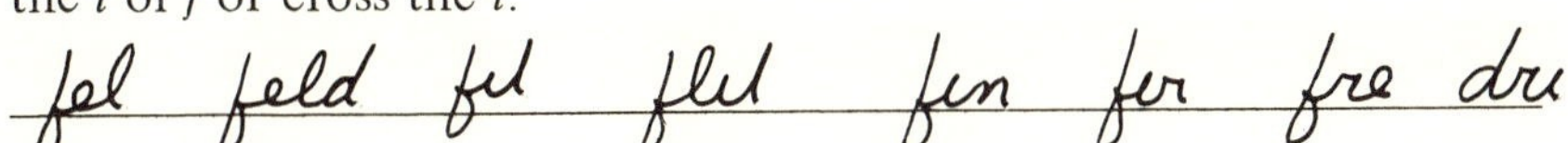

feel field fight flight fine fire free dry

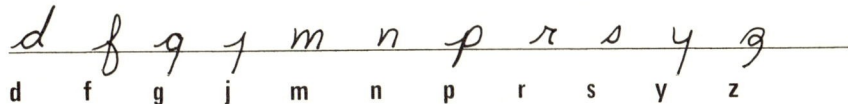

i	drv	lif	lit	lin	sin	tip	led
I	**drive**	**life**	**light**	**line**	**sign**	**type**	**lead (v.)**
les	lev	ner	ned	nit	pepl	len	
lease	**leave**	**near**	**need**	**night**	**people**	**lean**	
pris	red	rit	sezn	se	siz	jen	
price	**read**	**right**	**season**	**see-sea**	**size**	**Jean**	
ttl	trete	ses	eze	den	ej	sen	
title	**treaty**	**cease**	**easy**	**dean**	**edge**	**seen-scene**	

Learning tips. When an outline stands for more than one word, as in *see-sea,* the meaning of the sentence tells you the right word. (2) Do not use capital letters when writing proper names; put a check mark under proper names (see *Jean* above).

Sounds of hard *c* and *k*. Write longhand *c* for *k* and hard sounds of *c*.

cler	clen	cri	ce	cep	lic	blec	sec
clear	**clean**	**cry**	**key**	**keep**	**like**	**bleak**	**seek**
bic	cen	cit	slec	frec	cred		
bike	**keen**	**kite**	**sleek**	**freak**	**creed**		

Learning tip. The longhand *c* is used for all "cuh" sounds because it is much easier to write than *k*.

Abbreviating common words. To build notetaking speed, you will abbreviate a few common words. These time-savers are called *abbreviated words.*

Study the print and the outlines below until you can read the notes as fast as you can the print. Then cover the outlines and write the notes from print several times as fast as you can.

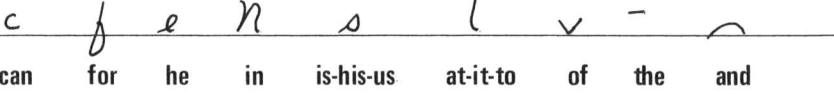

c	f	e	n	s	t	v	–	⌒
can	**for**	**he**	**in**	**is-his-us**	**at-it-to**	**of**	**the**	**and**

NOTES TO READ AND WRITE

Throughout this program, you will find sentences, letters, and other passages that will help you learn to apply the writing shortcuts. You will also find a key to these notes at the end of each chapter.

Read the notes until you can read them as fast as you can read the print. (If you can't make out a word after sounding it out, look at the key at the end of the chapter.) Then write your own notes quickly from the print passage. *Say each sentence to yourself as you write it.* Write each sentence from print until you can do so without hesitation.

1. - sez s fun, ⌒ - pris s rit.
2. jen s t tip - sun ⌒ lev t ner - ef v - feld.
3. i c led - pepl N - fil f - trele t ses fur.
4. t s - rit sezn t driv t - se.
5. c e se - lil lin v tip? i fel t s eze t red.
6. - lill s fre ⌒ cler, ⌒ e c les s feld t s f - sezn.
7. - flit i ned s t lev - feld t rit.
8. e c led - fre ⌒ eze lif.
9. i lic t cep - bic clen ⌒ dri.

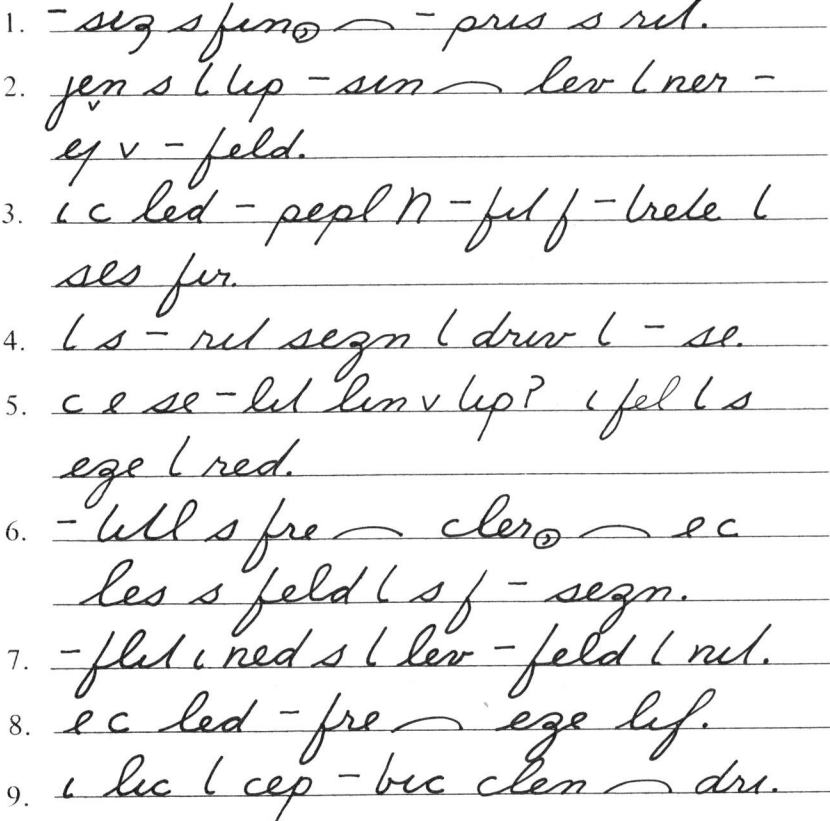

Learning tips. (1) Don't capitalize the first word in a sentence. (2) Use regular punctuation marks, but circle commas, apostrophes, and quotation marks.

NOTETAKING APPLICATIONS

1. Your *Handbook* includes a self-check on every writing shortcut in this text. With these self-checks, you can measure your own performance and take corrective action if needed. Turn to Unit 2 in your *Handbook* and complete the self-checks.

2. Use Tape 1 Side A from the *Notetaking Tape Library* to build your speed in notetaking. If these tapes are not available, your instructor will read the words and sentences in the text while you take notes. Leave your text open as an aid in taking down the notes.

3. If time permits, complete the optional applications at the end of Unit 2 in the *Handbook*.

KEY TO *NOTES TO READ AND WRITE*

1. The size is fine, and the price is right.
2. Jean is to type the sign and leave it near the edge of the field.
3. I can lead the people in the fight for the treaty to cease fire.
4. It is the right season to drive to the sea.
5. Can he see the light line of type? I feel it is easy to read.
6. The title is free and clear, and he can lease his field to us for the season.
7. The flight I need is to leave the field at night.
8. He can lead the free and easy life.
9. I like to keep the bike clean and dry.

WRITING STYLES AND NOTETAKING

You have learned to modify your writing style to eliminate extra writing strokes, and you have tried to make your notetaking outlines look like those in the book. Even so, your outlines will differ in some way from the text examples because your writing style is unique. To show that the writing shortcuts suggested can be used readily with various handwriting styles, several shorthand writers have written outlines for this text.

Chapter 3

WRITING SHORTCUTS

Sounds of short *e*. Omit *e* when the short sound of *e* occurs in the *body* of a word.

Cover the print of the first line of words and read the notes until you can read them easily. Then quickly write the outline of each word 3 times on a piece of lined paper. Follow the same procedure with the second line of words. Do not move ahead until you can read and write quickly all the words illustrating the sounds of short *e*.

nvr rde prs lft srv svrl fdrl bt

never ready press left serve several federal bet

sd ll lvl sl gt lt eg yt sns

said tell level sell get let egg yet sense

Learning tips. (1) The letter *e* has 2 basic sounds: long *e* as in *need* and *eat;* and short *e* as in *red, less,* and *never.* You write *e* when you hear the long *e* sound in words like *see, lease,* and *field.* To save writing strokes, omit *e* when the short sound of *e* occurs in the *body* of a word. (2) The short *e* in *egg* does not occur in the *body* of the word, therefore it is written.

Sounds of *a*. Write an apostrophe for all sounds of *a*.

With the print covered, read the notes for words illustrating the sounds of *a*. When you can read the notes fluently, cover the notes and leave the print visible. Now write the outline for each word. When finished, check your notes with those in the text. Are you remembering to omit extra beginning and ending strokes? Did you write the initial *p* correctly in *paper* and *place*? Rewrite any words you wrote incorrectly.

' 'bl d' l'br p'pr gl'd cl's c'l 'j

a able day labor paper glad class call age

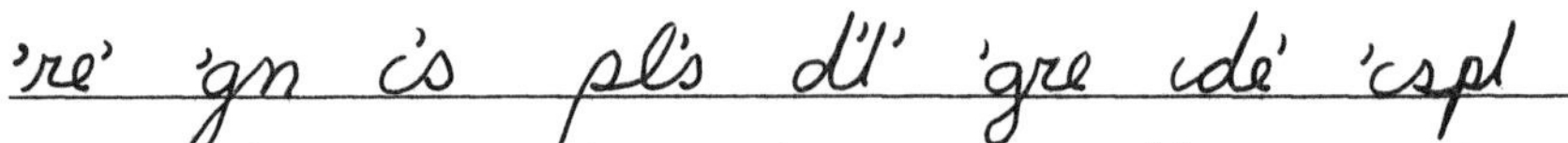

area again case place data agree idea accept

travel appear apply cause available late airliner

Learning tips. (1) You write the *a*-apostrophe for all sounds of *a*—the *a* sound in *able,* the *a* sound in *glad,* and the *a* sound in *call.* (2) Write the *a*-apostrophe first if the *a* sound comes first in a word. Write it last at all other times.

Sounds of short *i*. Make an *i*-dot above the line to show where the sound of short *i* occurs in a word.

Cover the print of each line of words and read the notes until you can read them as fast as you can read the print. Then write the outline for each word once, and read your own notes back.

give bill if did little written fill since kill

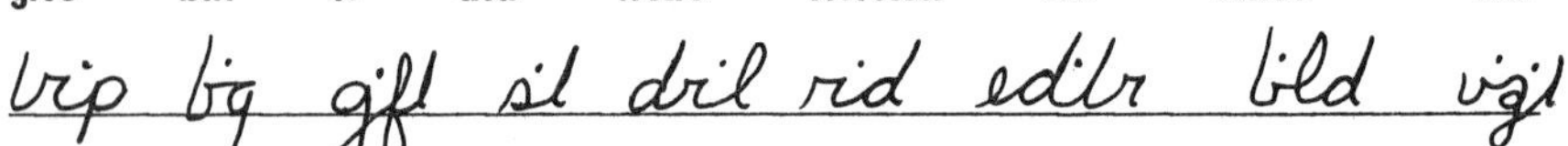

trip big gift sit drill rid editor build visit

Learning tip. The letter *i* has 2 sounds: long *i* as in *life* and *line;* and short *i* as in *if* and *fill.* You have learned to write the undotted *i* for long sounds of *i.*

Sounds of *o*. Write a comma on or below the line for sounds of *o*.

As you read each word illustrating the sounds of *o*, write the note for each word several times. After you have read and written the notes for all the words, you should be able to read and write them rapidly and accurately.

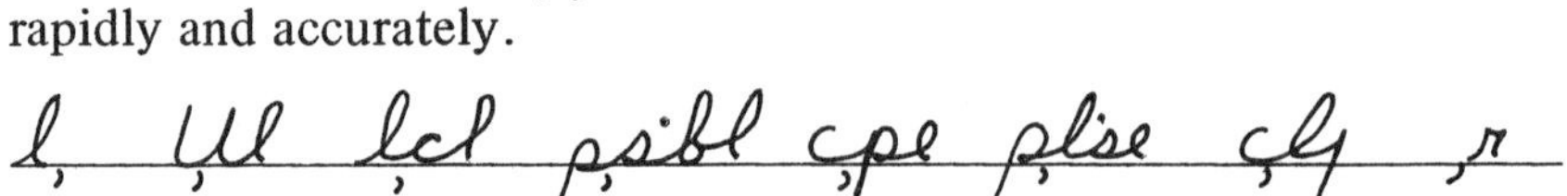

low total local possible copy policy college or

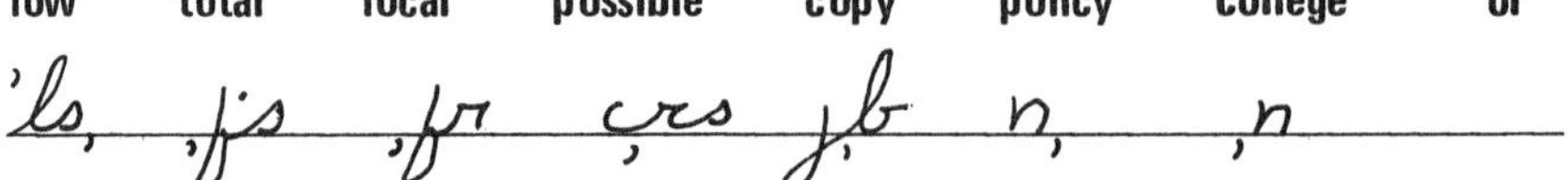

also office offer course job no-know on-own

Learning tip. Note that the *o*-comma is written for all sounds of *o*—the *o* in *total,* the *o* as in *off* or *bought,* and the *o* in *copy.*

Phrasing. Run common words together and write them as one word.

Read the notes for the following phrases with the print covered until you can read the notes as fast as you can the print. Then cover the notes and practice writing the phrases from the print. Check your notes with those in the text.

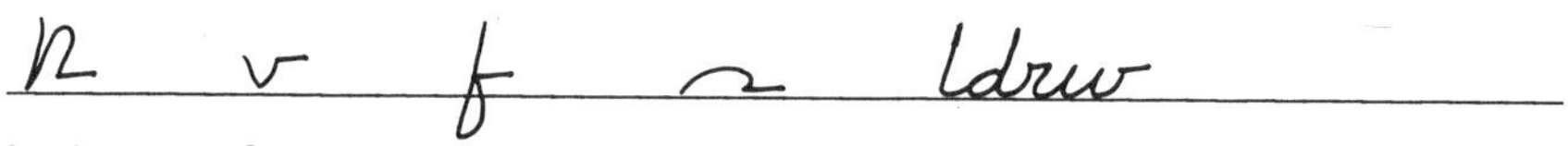

in the **of the** **for the** **and the** **to drive**

Learning tip. Phrasing is a matter of individual preference; therefore, you should consider the phrases in this book as suggestions. If phrasing is easy for you, then you may want to devise additional phrases. If, on the other hand, you find them hard to write and read, you should use fewer phrases.

NOTES TO READ AND WRITE

Read the following notes until you can read them without hesitation. Then turn to the key and write your own notes from the print. Say each sentence to yourself as you write it. Check your notes with those in the text.

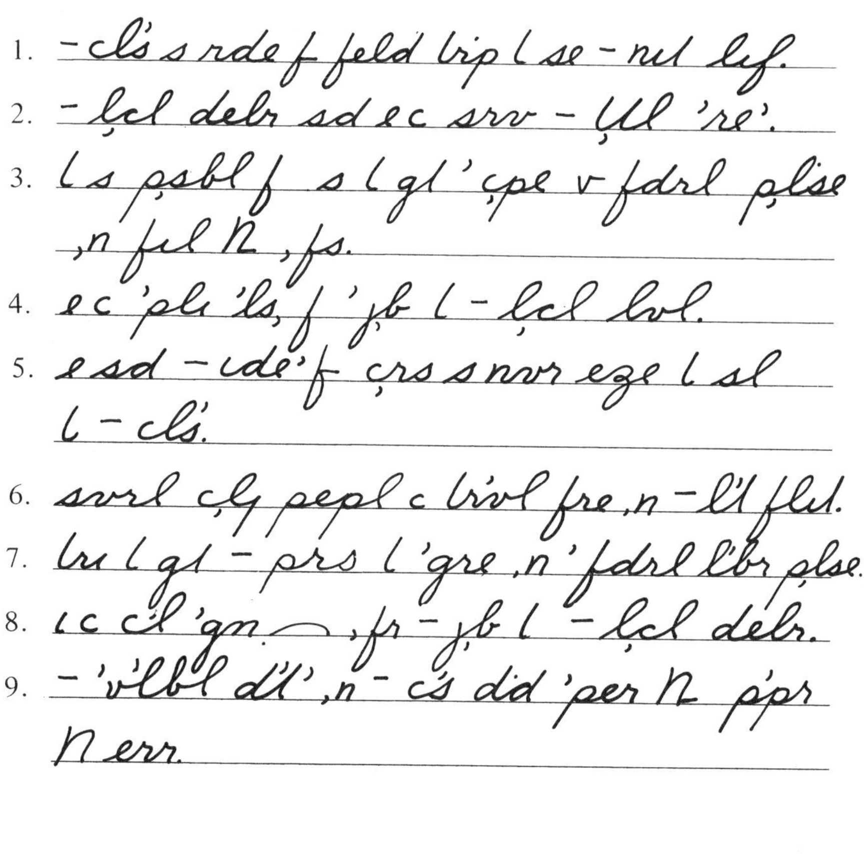

10. jen s gl'd l srv – c'z v pes.
11. tri l giv – cl's ' ltl ritn dril.
12. 'ritn plse ,n trvl s rde l giv l – editr.
13. tl jen l c'l l se if – flit lft – feld.
14. i n, t s psibl l 'gre ,n ' l, pris f jb.

NOTETAKING APPLICATIONS

1. Complete the self-checks in Unit 3 in your *Handbook*.
2. Use Tape 1 Side A from the *Notetaking Tape Library* to build speed. If the tapes are not available, your instructor will read the words and sentences to you while you take notes.
3. If time permits, complete the Optional Applications.

KEY TO *NOTES TO READ AND WRITE*

1. The class is ready for the field trip to see the night life.
2. The local dealer said he can serve the total area.
3. It is possible for us to get a copy of the federal policy on file in the office.
4. He can apply also for a job at the local level.
5. He said the idea for the course is never easy to sell to the class.
6. Several college people can travel free on the late flight.
7. Try to get the press to agree on a federal labor policy.
8. I can call again and offer the job to the local dealer.
9. The available data on the case did appear in the paper in error.
10. Jean is glad to serve the cause of peace.
11. Try to give the class a little written drill.
12. A written policy on travel is ready to give to the editor.
13. Tell Jean to call to see if the flight left the field.
14. I know it is possible to agree on a low price for the job.

Chapter 4

SETTING ACADEMIC GOALS

Many college freshmen are overwhelmed by the amount of study and reading they have to do. Maybe you have heard them complain, "In high school, I got good grades with hardly any homework. But here, most of my work is done on my own outside of class." It is no secret that many first-year college students have great difficulty until they learn to set their own academic goals and to plan their time in order to attain those goals.

What academic goals will you set for yourself? How much study time is likely to be required if you are to reach your goals?

Many college counselors advise students to use the following rule of thumb in setting their goals: For every credit hour taken, allow one hour of study per week outside of class for a grade of C; 2 hours of outside study per week for a B; and 3 hours per week for an A. Assume, for example, that you have enrolled for a total of 15 credits, and your goal is to get a B average. Here is how you would figure your total hours of school and study for a typical week in order to reach your goal:

Total hours in class for 15 credits	15
Hours of study required to average a grade of B (estimated at 2 hours per credit)	30
Total hours in class and for study	45

Of course, your "work week" would be even longer if you had a part-time job, went out for sports, or engaged in other activities. Whatever happened to the 40-hour week! Few students—or their parents—realize that a full-time college program can take more hours per week than a full-time job.

Bear in mind that the relationship between time spent studying and academic accomplishment suggested above will not apply to everyone in every situation. For example, if you are an efficient learner and are taking courses that are easy for you, less outside study time would be needed to attain your objectives.

Later chapters will give you many practical suggestions for increasing your learning skill and for using your study time to maximum advantage.

TO CONSIDER AND DISCUSS

1. Talk with a college student about the differences between academic work in high school and college. Be prepared to report your findings to the class.
2. Do you feel that setting academic goals helps improve achievement? Explain.

WRITING SHORTCUTS

Sounds of *u-oo*. Write a short, slanted, downward stroke on or below the line of writing to express all sounds of *u* and *oo*.

Cover the print and read the notes until you can read the outlines as fast as you can read the print. Then cover the outlines and practice writing them from print until you can write all the outlines in 30 seconds.

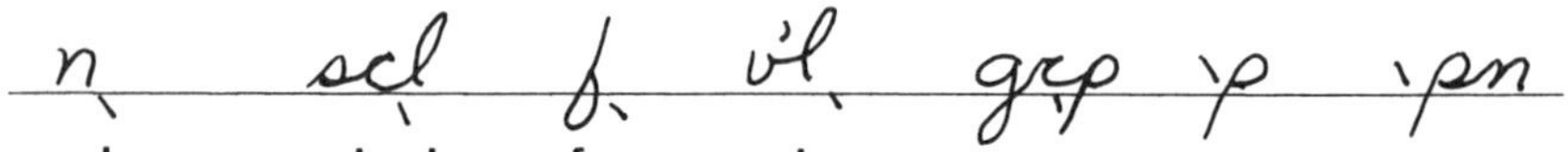

new-knew school few value group up upon

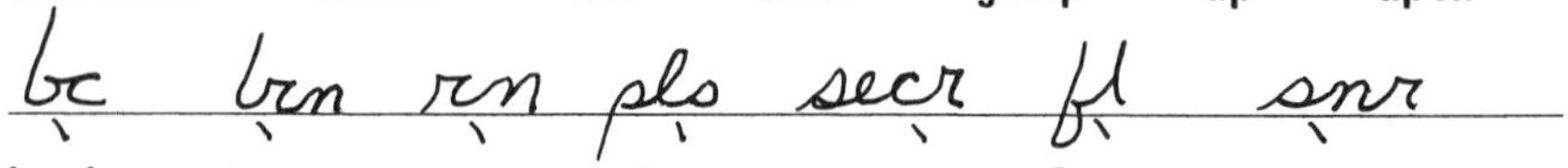

book turn run plus secure foot sooner

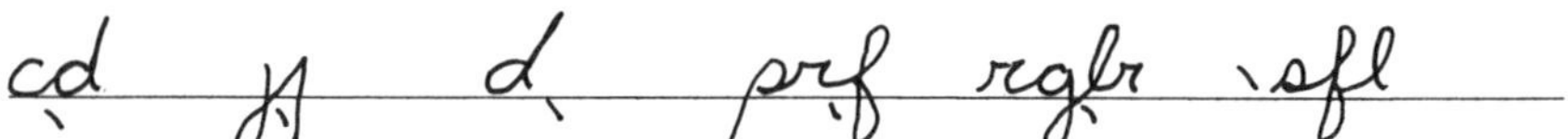

could judge due-dew proof regular useful

Sounds of *m*. Write a long, straight line on or above the line to express *m*.

Read the words illustrating the sound of *m*. When you can read the first line fluently, cover the print and write the outlines. Practice until you can write each word rapidly and accurately. Follow the same procedure for each line.

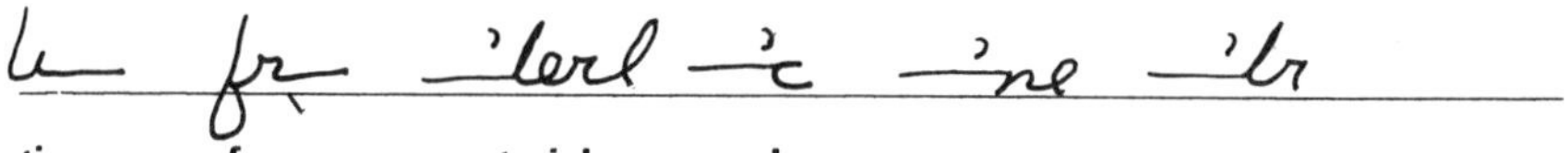

time from material make many matter

committee me might complete same member

meet money my market model mail-male

submit term may come

Learning tips. (1) Make the *m*-stroke long. It is the letter, *m,* stretched out into a straight line. (2) Did you note that the *m's* in *member* are joined with a slight jog? How would you write *memo*?

Syllable *ment*. Write the longhand *m* for the syllable *ment.*

Read the outlines quickly with the print covered. Then write each outline once and read your notes back to yourself.

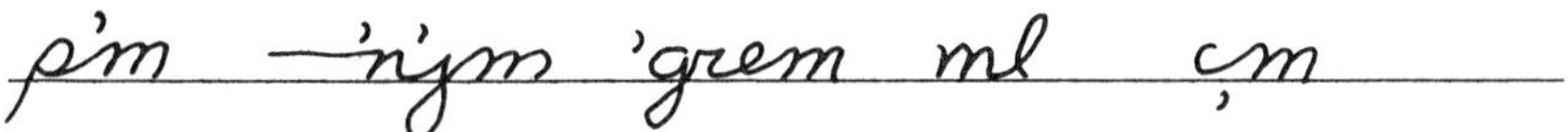

payment management agreement mental comment

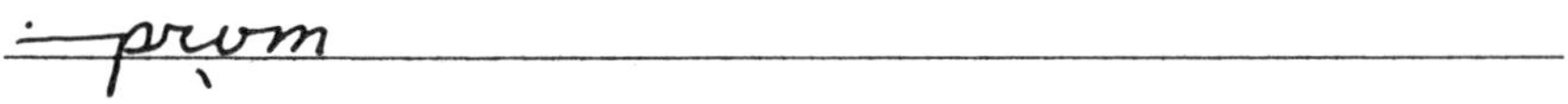

improvement

Adding *s* to root words. Join an upward, slanted, straight stroke to the last letter or symbol of a word to add *s*.

As you read each word illustrating this writing rule, write the root word first. Then write the root word again, adding the *s*-stroke. Follow this example as you practice:

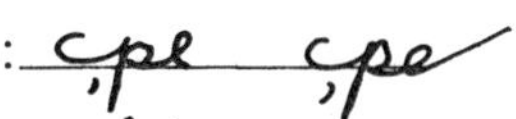

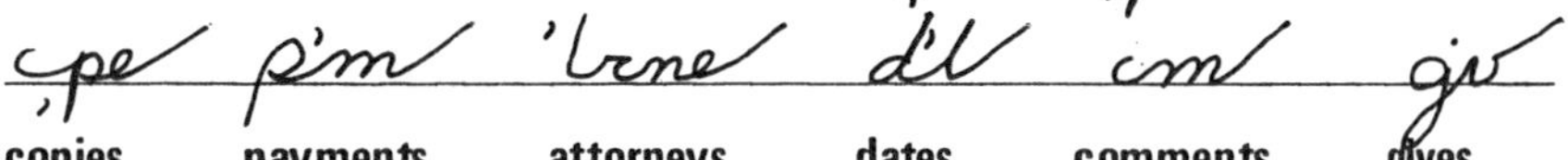

copies payments attorneys dates comments gives

fees members needs days ideas courses claims

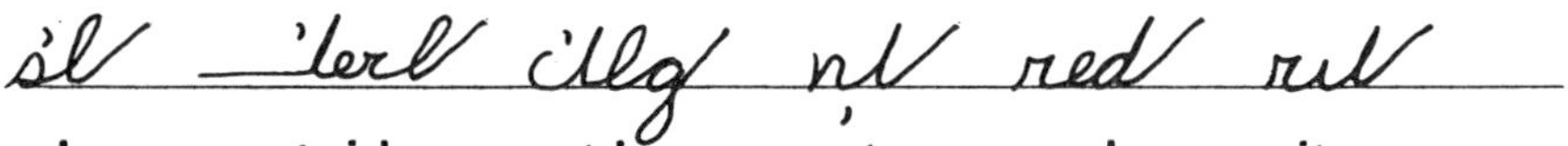

sales materials catalogs notes reads writes

Abbreviated words. The following commonly-used words must be memorized to help you build your notetaking speed. As you learn the outlines, practice writing each one 3 times.

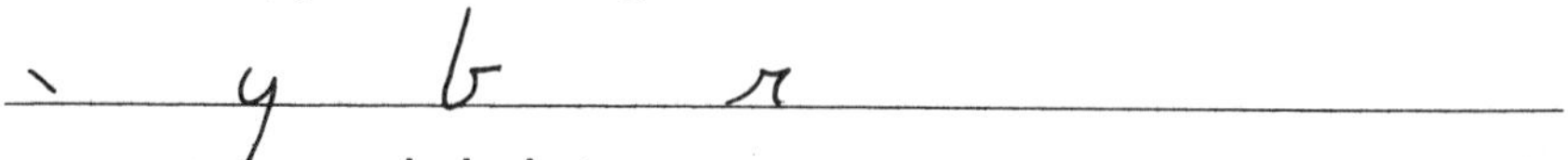

you your be-by-but are

Phrases. Here are some common phrases that will help you build your speed in taking notes.

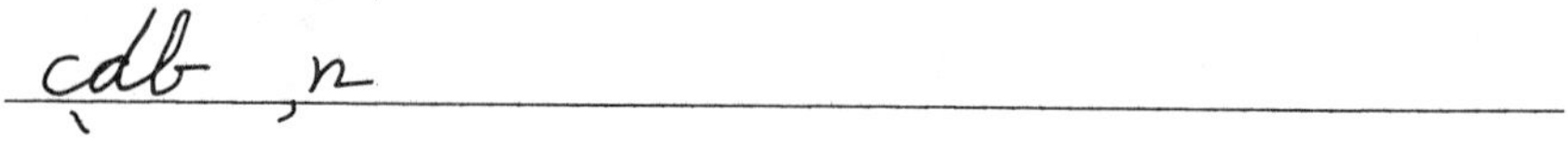

could be on the

NOTES TO READ AND WRITE

Read the following notes. If you cannot read a word, look at the print at the end of the chapter. When you can read the notes easily, turn to the print passage and write your notes from print. Read an entire sentence and then say it back to yourself as you write your notes. If you practice in this way, you will write your notes fluently; and you will train yourself to remember what you have read.

1. 
2. 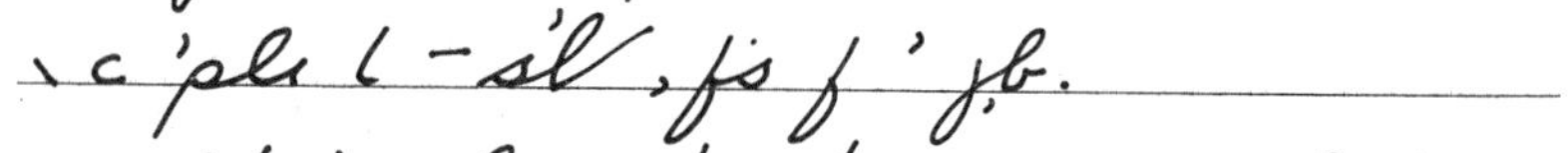
3. 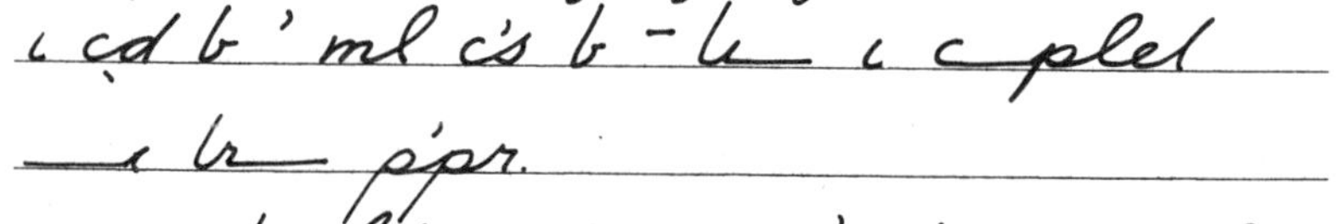
4. 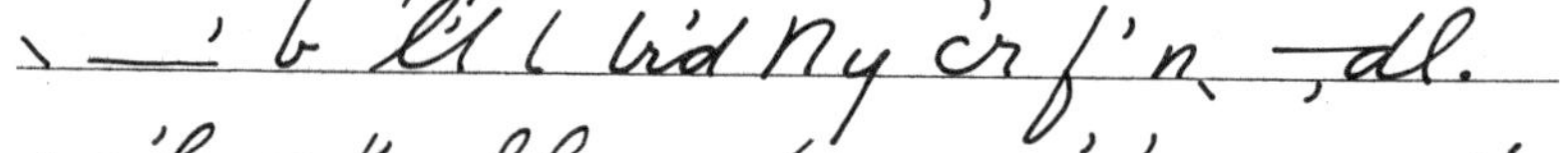
5. 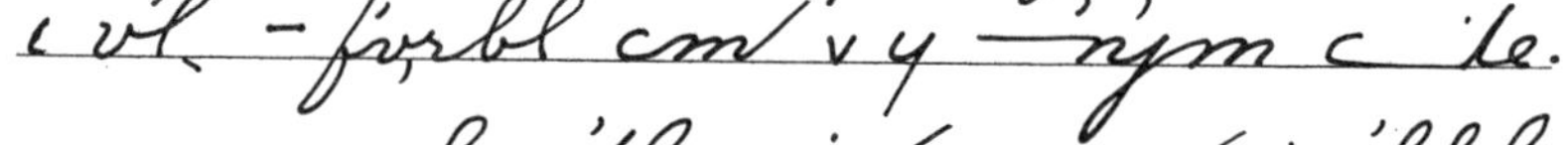
6. 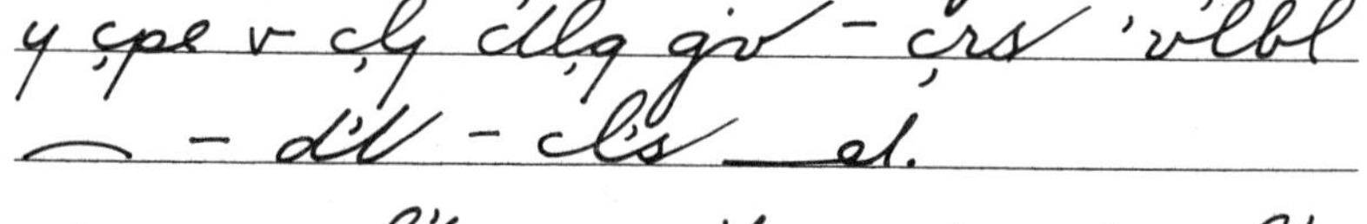
7. 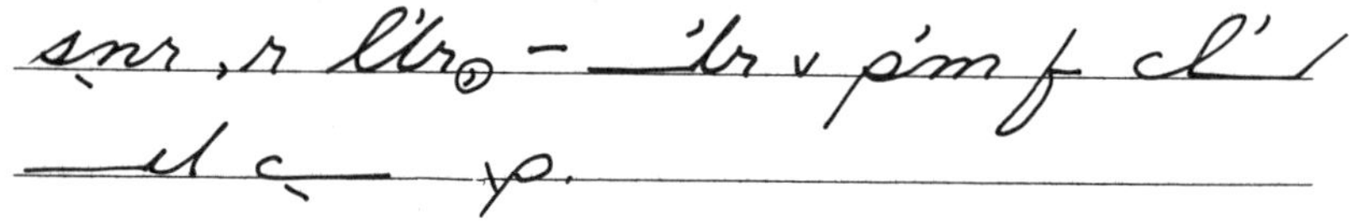

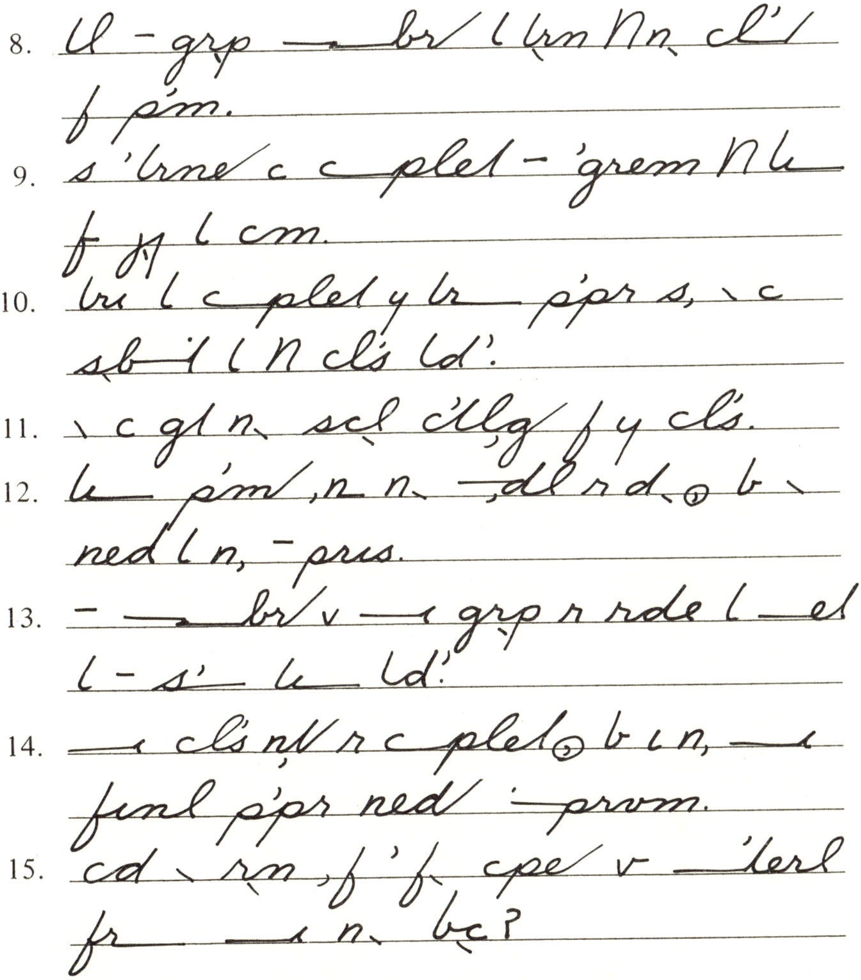

NOTETAKING APPLICATIONS

1. Turn to Unit 4 in your *Handbook* and complete the self-checks.
2. Use Tape 1 Side B from the *Notetaking Tape Library* to build your speed in notetaking. If these tapes are not available, have someone read the words and sentences to you while you take notes. Leave your text open as an aid in taking down the notes.
3. If time permits, complete the optional note-reading exercises at the end of Unit 4 in the *Handbook*.

KEY TO *NOTES TO READ AND WRITE*

1. I can give the editor a copy of the new book today.
2. You can apply to the sales office for a job.
3. I could be a mental case by the time I complete my term paper.
4. You may be late to trade in your car for a new model.
5. I value the favorable comments of your management committee.
6. Your copy of the college catalog gives the courses available and the dates the classes meet.
7. Sooner or later, the matter of payment for the claims might come up.
8. Tell the group members to turn in new claims for payment.
9. His attorneys can complete the agreement in time for the judge to comment.
10. Try to complete your term paper so you can submit it in class today.
11. You can get new school catalogs for your class.
12. Time payments on the new model are due, but you need to know the price.
13. The members of my group are ready to meet at the same time today.
14. My class notes are complete, but I know my final paper needs improvement.
15. Could you run off a few copies of the material from my new book?

Chapter 5

LEARNING TO LEARN

A recent national survey showed that 4 out of 5 college freshmen felt they had not been taught study skills in high school—that they had not been taught how to learn.[1]

Do you study efficiently? Have you mastered the skills needed to learn more in less time—and to retain new learnings longer? If so, you are most fortunate, because your future in school and on a job will depend on your skill in absorbing new ideas and skills.

HOW TO STUDY EFFICIENTLY

Take the first step in learning to study more efficiently by comparing your study habits and techniques with those used by the best students. If you are an efficient student, you—

Organize your time. The skillful student schedules time carefully and then follows the schedule. Many use an hour-by-hour schedule to remind themselves of when, what, and how long to study each subject. Of course, your schedule must be flexible to allow extra time for exams, library time for term papers, and the like. Furthermore, your schedule should be realistic. It should provide time for leisure activities, a job if you have one, and other out-of-school activities.

When is the best time of day to study? That is up to you. Keep in mind, however, that most people are far more efficient in the morning than at night. You will probably find that you can accomplish more in 30 minutes at 8:30 a.m. than you can in one hour at 8:30 p.m. Furthermore, the more you get done early in the day, the more time you will have in the evenings for phone calls, leisure activities, and special projects.

Make productive use of unscheduled time. Even with a precise schedule as suggested above, you will frequently find short periods—sometimes only 5 or 10 minutes—when you can study productively. For example, a 5-minute interval before a class lecture begins can be used to review and perfect your lecture notes from a previous class. This short review while the lecture is fresh in your mind may be equivalent to a 30-minute review of that same material at a later date.

[1] Alexander W. Astin, Margo R. King, and Gerald T. Richardson, *The American Freshman: National Norms for Fall 1975* (Los Angeles: Laboratory for Research in Higher Education, 1976), p. 42.

Review regularly. There are 2 very good scientific reasons why you should review regularly. First, we begin to forget what we have been exposed to soon after the exposure. Second, the longer we have been exposed to something, the better we retain it. In some ways, learning is like getting a suntan. The effects of one exposure soon begin to fade. Repeated exposure, however, helps to retain a suntan as well as ideas you have learned.

Make hard choices. To study efficiently, you must be prepared to give up or postpone other activities that may be more amusing and pleasant than studying. When it is time to study, can you flick off the TV without watching a few more moments to sample tonight's episode? This does not mean you have to give up TV. Again, be realistic. It does mean, though, that you should schedule your TV viewing just as you schedule your study time. If you set aside time on your weekly schedule for your favorite show, then you can enjoy it without feeling guilty about not studying.

Find a good place to work. Obviously, you don't need a carpeted room lined with books or an isolated monk's cell in order to study efficiently. But you do need a nook somewhere that you reserve for studying—a corner of a room, a basement retreat, or any other place that is free of distractions.

What about equipment? Of course, you need a good work surface, a chair, and good light. But you don't need a walnut desk and an executive chair. Use your creativity to design your study nook. A sheet of smooth plywood on a couple of supports can serve as a desk. If you prefer to study in an easy chair, a Masonite or plywood "study board" will be useful.

Get to work. Sounds trite? Maybe so, but the real test of your self-discipline comes when your schedule says, "Time to study."

Can you find countless excuses for delay? If you don't get right to work, can you easily talk yourself into putting study off altogether? If so, a regular "getting-ready-to-study" routine can often help. For example, if you are a compulsive pencil sharpener, sharpen all your pencils just *before* it is time for you to begin to study. This activity gives a distinct break between all other activities and study. A unique act reserved as a "pre-study routine" helps many students get started. And a pre-study routine also alerts others that you are not to be disturbed.

Tackle hard assignments first. If you start with easy assignments, you may run out of time and energy before you get to your difficult subjects. Then too, finishing up a hard assignment gives you a "lift" that can help you breeze through the easy assignments. So, if you have a choice to make, work on your hardest subjects first.

Anticipate materials needed. An excuse for not studying is to "forget" to check out that needed book from the library or to "leave" your notebook with the assignment in your locker. Make sure you have everything you need before you start to study. Round up paper, pen, colored pencils for underlining, books—everything you will need—as part of your "getting-ready-to-study routine."

Use suitable strategies. Skill subjects are learned more efficiently when studied daily for short periods of time. For example, most people can learn much more foreign language in 3, 40-minute sessions than they can in one study session of 120 minutes. Non-skill subjects like history and economics, on the other hand, can be studied for longer periods without a serious loss in learning efficiency.

STRATEGIES FOR LEARNING NOTETAKING

Because notetaking is a skill, you should try to set aside a few minutes each day for outside-of-class study and practice. Here are additional practical suggestions:

1. Begin to use your notetaking skill in taking lecture and reading notes. By now you can write many thousands of words with the writing shortcuts you have learned. The more you use these writing shortcuts, the sooner you will respond automatically to words you read and hear.
2. If they are available to you, use the cassettes from the *Notetaking Tape Library* to help you build your skill.
3. Practice your notetaking with another student occasionally. One can read words, sentences, and other material while the other practices writing.
4. "Think" notetaking. When you see a sign or a billboard, think how the outlines of the words should be written. When you hear lyrics to a song or a radio commercial, think how the outlines of the words would look. Practice "processing" all incoming messages into notetaking outlines.

SUMMARY

You learn what you practice. In this chapter you have been given suggestions for building your skill in learning. The next step in learning these skills is to use them—to practice and perfect them and to find out which suggestions work best for you. Resolve now to apply the following suggestions as you study this coming week:

1. Schedule your time. If you find you cannot stick to your schedule, analyze your difficulty. Then draw up a new schedule and try again.

2. Use those short unscheduled breaks. Don't waste those 5- and 10-minute intervals.
3. Review regularly so that you reinforce your learning before it begins to fade. Remember how you reinforce a suntan.
4. Make hard choices. At the end of this week, be able to name at least 3 activities you postponed in order to stick to your study schedule.
5. Reexamine your study place. Try to find a nook that you reserve for study alone.
6. Begin work on schedule. Keep a record of any activities that prevented you from beginning your study periods on schedule.
7. At the end of this week, be able to cite at least 3 instances of when you did your hardest assignment first.
8. Keep a record of the number of times your study period was interrupted or postponed because you did not have on hand the materials needed for the assignment.
9. Use learning strategies most appropriate for the subject you are studying.

TO CONSIDER AND DISCUSS

1. Which suggestion for improving your study efficiency do you feel will help you most? Explain why.
2. What factor or activity most frequently diverts you from studying? Explain, and be ready to discuss how you think you can control the distraction.
3. Give 2 reasons for doing difficult assignments first.
4. In what 2 ways is learning like getting a suntan?

NOTES TO READ AND WRITE

The following sentences will help you to review the writing shortcuts in the preceding chapters. No new writing rules are presented. Read the following notes until you can read them without hesitation. Then turn to the key at the end of the chapter and write your own notes from the print.

1. 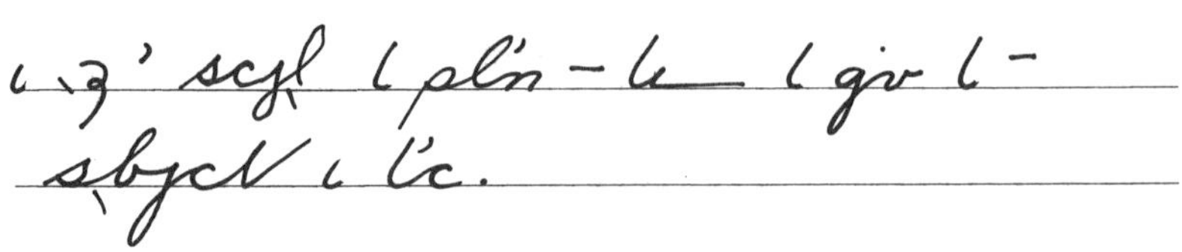

2. – pris v ecn_e ċr s vre l, ⊙ ⌒ – delr gv_e ' fr pris f _ı ċr.

3. – dlf bsbl g_ cb sl ld',r l_r,.

4. – r_ s lry enff __br/ v c_le.

5. ı rl ' nl l gv – jnrl_nyr _ı çm/ ,n _br.

6. c ↘ ern enf_ne l br 10 gln/ v l, ld gs f y ċr?

7. lnul ıc lıp⌒ prfred – rf drfl v _ı fınl lr_ ppr f çrs.

8. c ↘ c_plet – bç s, ↘ c lrn l N b – l_ – lıbrre clz/?

9. _ı ċr_ b bel ↘ p⊙ b ı nls ↘ se_ l luc l rud N l.

10. nlfı_e b fnıf ↘ _s y pln ,r ıf l s l ruv ll.

11. ıf ↘ br y lcl f g_ ld⊙ ↘ _ gl ' sel cls l – feld.

12. N ccbc ıgv ↘ r_ne rspe/ f l, clre_el/.

13. 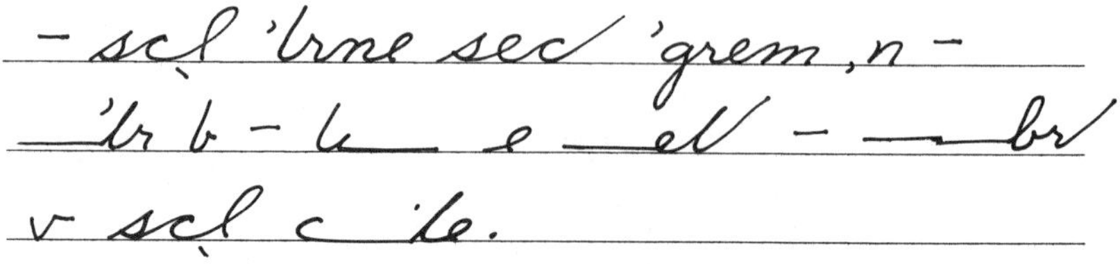

NOTETAKING APPLICATIONS

1. Turn to Unit 5 and complete the self-checks.
2. Use Tape 1 Side B to build your speed in notetaking.
3. If time permits, complete the Optional Application at the end of Unit 5.

KEY TO *NOTES TO READ AND REVIEW*

1. I use a schedule to plan the time to give to the subjects I take.
2. The price of the economy car is very low, and the dealer gave me a fair price for my car.
3. The date for the baseball game can be set today or tomorrow.
4. The room is large enough for the members of the committee.
5. I wrote a note to give the general manager my comments on the matter.
6. Can you earn enough money to buy 10 gallons of low-lead gas for your car?
7. Tonight I can type and proofread the rough draft of my final term paper for the course.
8. Can you complete the book so you can turn it in by the time the library closes?
9. My car may be beat up, but I notice you seem to like to ride in it.
10. Notify me by phone if you miss your plane or if it is to arrive late.
11. If you buy your ticket for the game today, you may get a seat close to the field.
12. In the cookbook I gave you are many recipes for low-calorie meals.
13. The school attorney seeks agreement on the matter by the time he meets the members of the school committee.

Chapter 6

THE MODERN TEXTBOOK

Most of your reading in school is probably done in textbooks. Have you ever examined a textbook's various parts carefully? If you do, you will become a better textbook reader and a better notemaker.

WHAT'S IN YOUR TEXT BOOK?

Each part of a textbook has a function to serve. Here are the major parts and the functions of each:

The title page. In addition to the title of the book, you'll find the authors' names and their professional affiliations on this page. With this information, you can make judgments about the qualifications of the authors. At the bottom of the title page is the publisher's name and location.

Copyright page. Usually found on the back of the title page, the copyright page gives the date of publication. In fields where knowledge advances rapidly, the publication date is obviously important. For example, a 10-year old text in physics is very much out-of-date.

Preface or foreword. Often ignored by readers, these brief statements give important information. The author usually tells the purpose of the book, gives instructions for its use, and explains the teaching approach used.

Table of contents. Here you will find an outline of the entire book. This complete list of the parts of the book gives page numbers for each part. In most texts, chapter subheads are also listed.

Chapter organization. Aids to learning and remembering are included in many texts. Do you use them to your advantage? The type styles and sizes used in major headings and subheadings show the organization of the material, and they suggest the key points in a chapter. Graphs, charts, tables, and pictures often clarify the points made in the text. Chapter summaries condense the author's ideas. Lists of other books (a bibliography) at the end of a chapter or at the end of a book lead you to other sources of information about the subject.

Index. Here you will find, arranged in alphabetical order, a list of names, topics, places, and other specific information. A good index enables you to locate readily the subject or item that you seek.

TO CONSIDER AND DISCUSS

Using a textbook from one of your other classes, write a brief report on the following:

1. The purpose or purposes of the book.
2. Describe the kinds of learning aids you find and indicate how they have helped you.
3. Indicate how the chapter summaries have helped you.

Use as many notetaking outlines as you can in preparing your report.

WRITING SHORTCUTS

Syllables *con-coun.* Write a capital *C* for *con* and *coun.*

Read the following words. Try to read them as fast as you can read the print. Then write each of the outlines and read them back. If any of your notes are difficult to read, rewrite them and read them again.

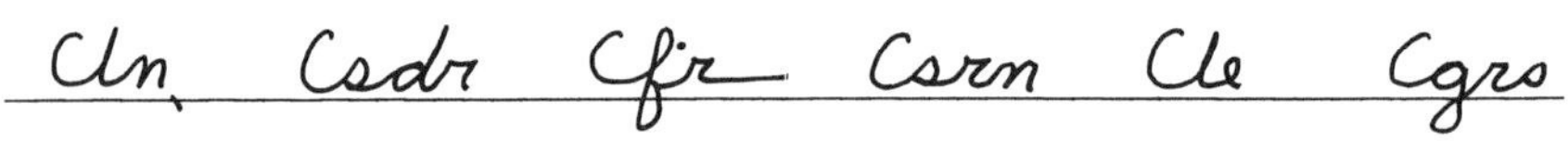

continue **consider** **confirm** **concern** **county** **congress**

Prefixes *be, de, re.* Omit the *e* in the prefixes, *be, de,* and *re.*

As you read each outline, practice writing it until you can do so accurately and rapidly. Say the word each time you write it.

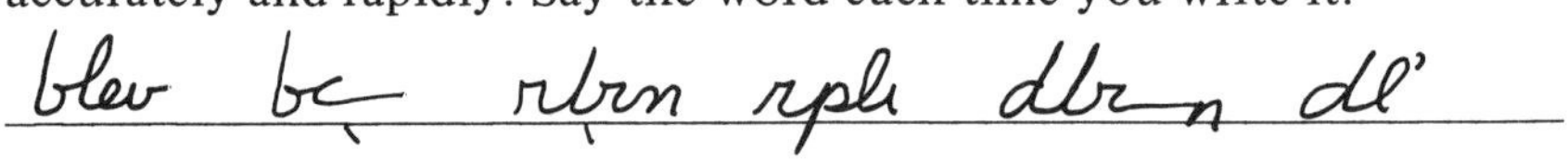

believe **become** **return** **reply** **determine** **delay**

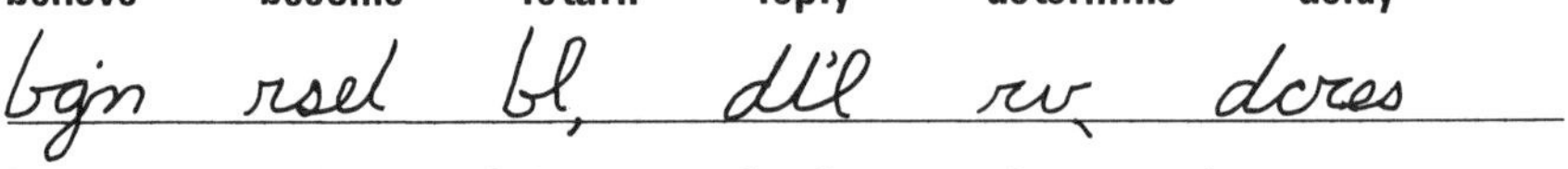

begin **receipt** **below** **detail** **review** **decrease**

The *shun* sounds. A short downward stroke under the last letter or symbol of a word adds the *shun* sound and the *preceding vowel* sound.

Cover the print and read the words until you can read them easily and without hesitation.

direction **nation-notion** **section** **edition** **operation**

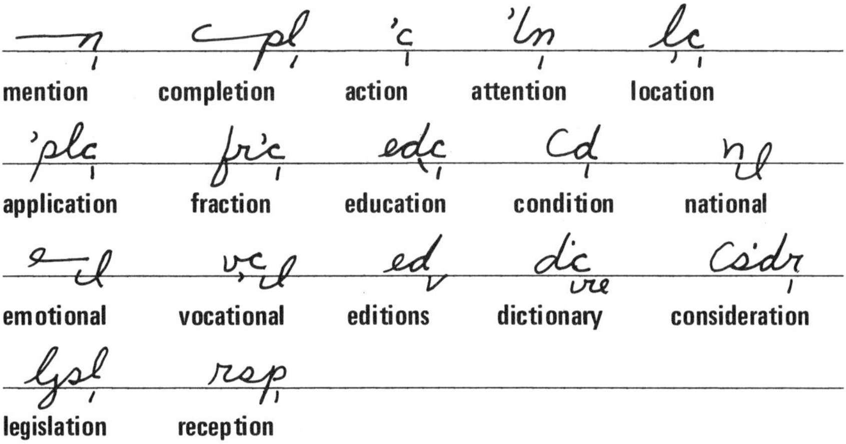

Learning tip. Remember that the *shun* stroke also stands for any vowel sound that immediately precedes the *shun* sound. For example, the *shun* stroke in *education* stands for *ation;* the *shun* stroke in *completion* stands for *etion,* and the *shun* in *edition* stands for *ition.* Note that additional endings may be added easily to the *shun* stroke in words like *dictionary, emotional,* and *national.*

Scribble-writing. In order to take notes readily, you must move your hand rapidly and write without hesitating. "Scribble-writing" will greatly increase your writing speed. To scribble-write, you keep your eyes on the outlines in the text as you write them on a separate piece of paper. Because you are not looking at your paper, you simply write one outline over the previous one—you do not move your hand across the page as you write. Say the words as you write them. Your notes will look something like this:

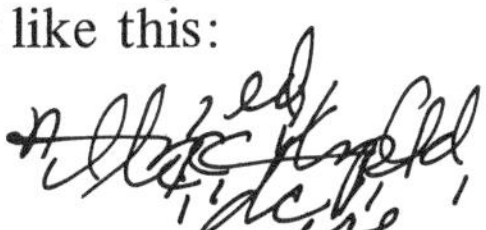

Increase your writing rate on the *shun* words by scribble-writing each word 3 times.

Abbreviated words. Memorize the following abbreviated words so that when you hear them you can write them automatically. Write each outline 3 times as you say the word.

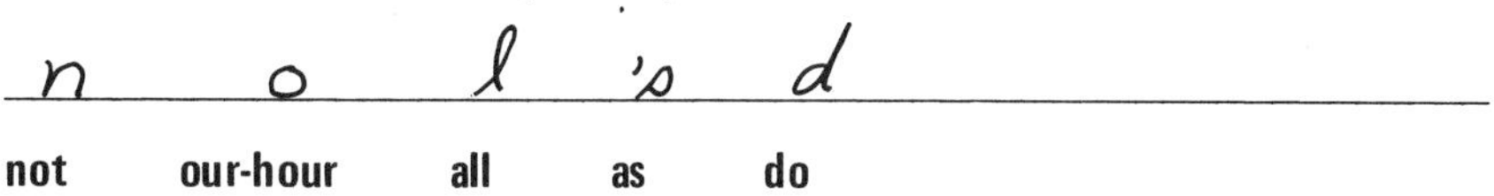

Phrases. If the following common phrases are easy for you to read, use them to save writing strokes.

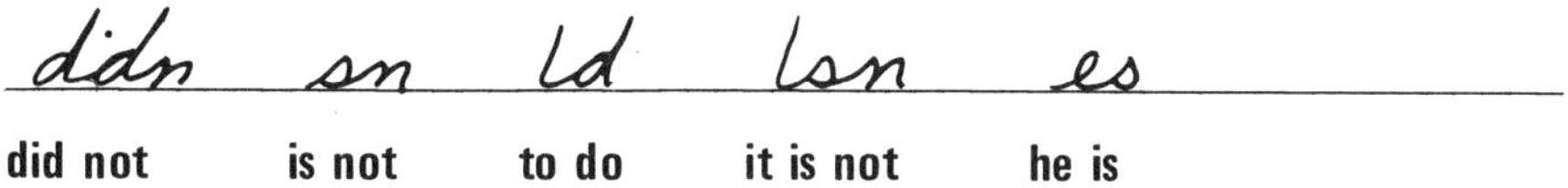

NOTES TO READ AND WRITE

Read the following notes until you can read them easily. If you cannot read a word, look at the key at the end of this chapter. When finished, turn to the printed key at the end of this chapter and write the sentences until you can do so fluently.

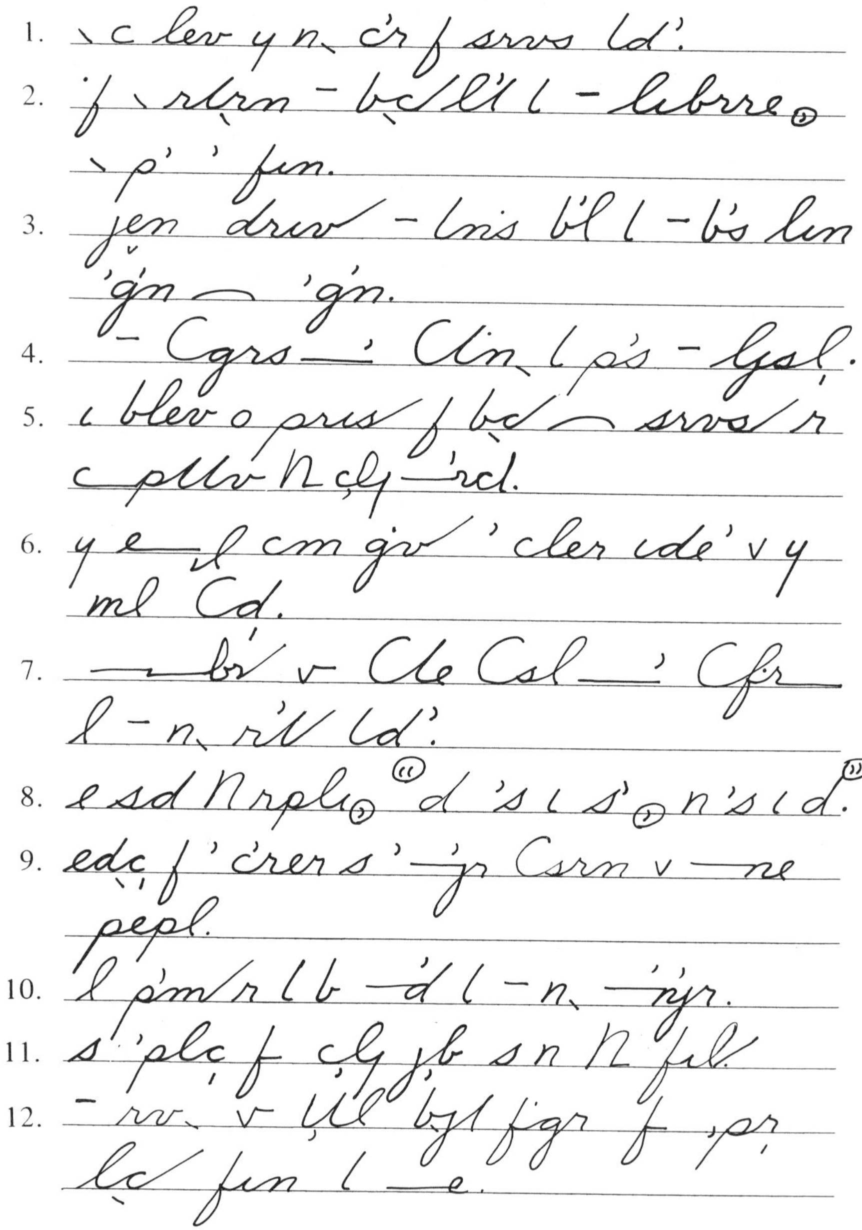

NOTETAKING APPLICATIONS

1. Complete the self-checks in Unit 6 in your *Handbook.*
2. Use Tape 2 Side A from the *Notetaking Tape Library* to build speed. If the tapes are not available, your instructor will read the words and sentences to you while you take notes.
3. If time permits, complete the Optional Applications.

KEY TO *NOTES TO READ AND WRITE*

1. You can leave your new car for service today.
2. If you return the books late to the library, you pay a fine.
3. Jean drives the tennis ball to the base line again and again.
4. The Congress may continue to pass the legislation.
5. I believe our prices for books and services are competitive in the college market.
6. Your emotional comment gives a clear idea of your mental condition.
7. Members of the county council may confirm all the new rates today.
8. He said in reply, "Do as I say, not as I do."
9. Education for a career is a major concern of many people.
10. All payments are to be made to the new manager.
11. His application for the college job is not in the files.
12. The review of the total budget figure for the operation looks fine to me.

Chapter 7

A NOTETAKING APPROACH TO READING

When you pick up something to read, you make decisions—either consciously or unconsciously—about your purpose. For example, your purpose is usually amusement when you read an article about your favorite celebrity or sport. When you read a textbook, however, your purpose is to master the author's ideas and concepts. In many of your courses, this kind of study-reading will occupy most of your study time and will be the source of much of what you learn: This intensive reading will also originate most of the notes you take.

THE 2A4R METHOD FOR STUDY-READING

Many students find that 6 logical steps help them to learn and remember what they read. The steps, known as the 2A4R method, are as follows: (1) analyze the task to be done, (2) ask questions, (3) read in detail, (4) recite, (5) record (make notes), and (6) review. Each step in this approach is described below:

Analyze the task to be done. Only if you analyze what's to be done can you plan your approach, budget your time, and check your progress toward your goals. And yet, many students overlook this vital first step. Plan to take the following steps to analyze your next reading assignment:

1. Read the first paragraph carefully. You will often find the central purpose of the assignment in that passage.
2. Turn to the end of the chapter and read the chapter summary. With this summary in mind, it is easier to see the relationships among the ideas that are presented.
3. If there are "questions for further study and discussion" at the end of the chapter, read them next. They usually suggest the main points in the assignment.
4. Then read the major headings and subheadings. These headings—in your own words—will probably be the major headings in your notes.
5. Remember the Chinese proverb: "One picture is worth a thousand words." Don't skip the illustrations, charts, and graphs. They usually give information on the main points.

When you have finished this survey, you should have a good analysis of the assignment. You will know how it relates to what you have read before, how it bears on lectures and class discussion, and what precisely is expected of you.

Ask questions about the topic that you feel should be answered in your reading. This is a very important and often little-understood step in reading for maximum efficiency. When you ask your own questions about what you are reading, you become an active participant in the reading process.

Use your notetaking skill to write questions down as they occur to you. Some questions will arise in your mind as you analyze the chapter; others will occur to you as you begin to read the assignment in detail.

Read in detail. Start by reading a short section of an assignment. Read to answer your own questions and those at the end of the passage. Look particularly for the author's main ideas. Most paragraphs include only one major idea, and in many cases it is found in the first sentence. If you are studying your own text, you may want to underline the main idea in each paragraph.

After reading each section, STOP. Then *recite* to check to see if you have learned what you have read.

Recite. Demonstrate to yourself that you understood and can recall what you have read by reciting in your own words the author's main ideas and supporting examples. Can you answer your questions about the passage? Does the passage help to answer questions at the end of the chapter? If so, you are ready to *record.* If you are unable to recall what you have read, go back and reread the passage.

Record. Using your notetaking skill, record the author's ideas in your own words and answer your own questions. Write only on the right half of your notebook page. Then on the left half of the page, jot down questions that might be asked about the passage. You will find suggestions for outlining and recording your notes in Chapter 9.

Review. After you have completed reading the entire assignment in short segments, cover the right side of your notes, leaving the questions exposed. Then answer each question to yourself, using the author's main points. Be sure that you can also cite examples for those questions that may end with ". . . give examples." If you can't answer a question you have written down, review your notes opposite that question.

2A4R IN ACTION

To illustrate how the 2A4R method works, try the following example. Your economics professor has assigned a 20-page chapter on business cycles. On the basis of your preview and analysis of the entire assignment, you develop many questions you will try to answer in your detailed reading. Among your questions are these:

1. Because the term "inflation" occurs in several headings, you conclude that it must play a significant role in business cycles. Your questions: Are business cycles caused by inflation? If so, how? Or is inflation caused by business cycles?
2. You find this question at the end of the chapter: "How does moderate inflation causes problems?" You conclude that inflation must be a serious problem; otherwise, why the question. The question in the text prompts you to jot down questions of your own: Inflation, a problem for whom? What kind of problems?

As you read, you run across the following paragraph:

> Moderate inflation may temporarily increase business profits, but in the long run it causes many problems. A retailer may be able to sell his inventory at higher prices than he anticipated. However, his costs for new merchandise and for salaries usually climb as prices rise. As a result, his profit margins begin to disappear. The business man is particularly subject to this "profit squeeze" if he is in a competitive business where his volume would decline if he raised prices. As salaries of his employees rise and the cost of merchandise goes up, the business man finds his profits squeezed between constantly rising costs and competitive prices.

Here is an answer you have been looking for. After you read the paragraph, you recite the main idea. Then you jot it down together with supporting material answering your questions.

If you picked the first sentence as the main idea and wrote it down in your own words, you are correct. Congratulations! Did you notice how the other sentences in the paragraph relate to the main idea? They give you more information about the author's key point. After the author states his main idea, he uses the example that begins in the second sentence to illustrate what he means. He shows precisely how mild inflation causes problems in the long run. He answers the questions you raised under (2) above. Incidentally, you also make special note of the term "profit squeeze" under "What kind of problems?" This vivid term may help to jog your memory about how inflation affects the business man.

TO CONSIDER AND DISCUSS

1. What key words does 2A4R stand for?
2. Give 3 reasons why it is important to analyze a reading assignment before beginning to read in detail.
3. What procedure can you use to become a more active reader?

WRITING SHORTCUTS

Letter *h*. Write a short dash ‾ to express the sound of *h*.

Cover the print and read the notes below until you can read the outlines as fast as you can read the print. Then cover the outlines and practice writing them from print until you can write all the outlines rapidly.

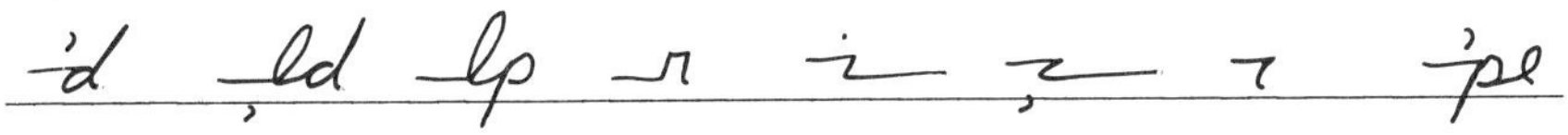

had **hold** **help** **her** **him** **home** **high** **happy**

hotel **hope** **helpful** **held** **here** **who** **happen**

Learning tips. (1) Make a slight jog when joining *h* to *m* in words like *him* and *home.* (2) Note how the *h* is joined to the long *i* in *high*, the *t* in *hotel*, and the *p* in *hope.*

Sounds of *sh*. Write an *h*-dash through *s* to express *sh* sounds.

As you read each word illustrating the sounds of *sh*, write each outline several times. When you have completed all words, you should be able to read and write them rapidly and accurately.

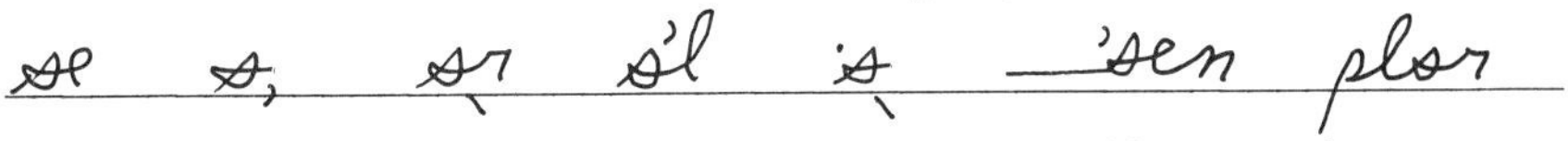

she **show** **sure** **shall** **issue** **machine** **pleasure**

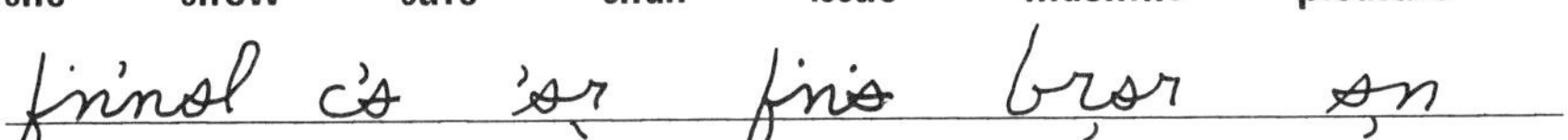

financial **cash** **assure** **finish** **brochure** **shown-shone**

Sounds of *th*. Join the *h*- dash to the *t* to express *th* sounds.

Read the following words. When you can read the first line fluently, cover the notes and write each outline as you read from the print. Practice until you can write each word rapidly and accurately. Follow the same procedure for each line.

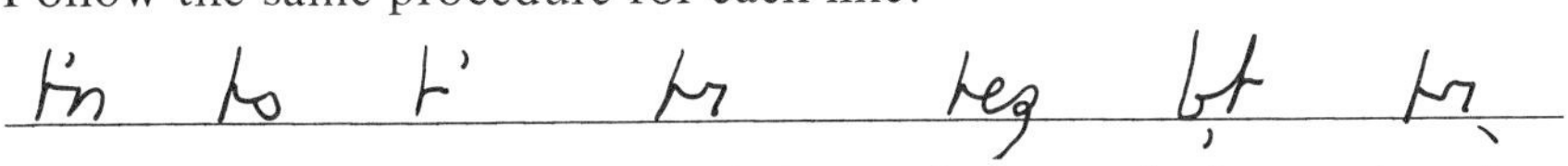

than **this** **they** **there-their** **these** **both** **through**

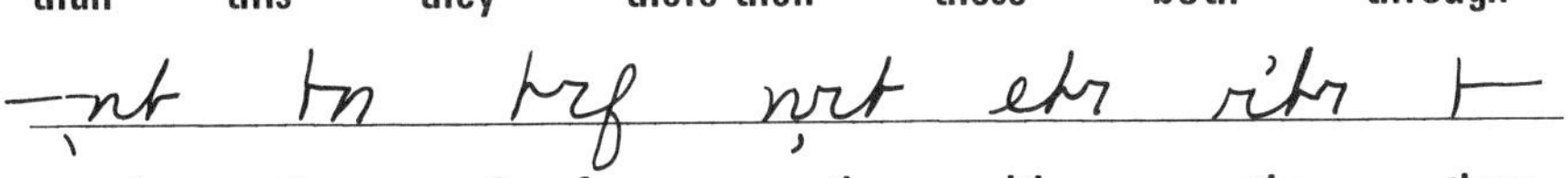

month **then** **therefore** **north** **either** **rather** **them**

Learning tip. Some writers prefer to cross the *t* to make the *th* combination:

Sounds of *ch*. Write an *h*- dash through *c* to express *ch*. 

When *ch* is the first sound in a word, write the *c* first and then write the *h*-dash through the *c* (see *cheer,* below). When *ch* occurs in the body of a word or at the end of a word, write the *h*-dash as an extension of the preceding letter and write the *c* through the extended *h*- dash.

As you read each word below, write the outline until you can write it without hesitation. Practice reading and writing each word until all are mastered.

cheer check charge children teacher touch attach

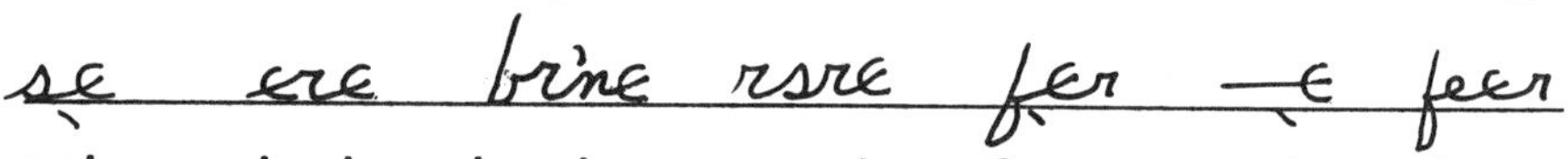

such church branch research future much feature

Abbreviated words. The following words must be memorized to help you build your notetaking speed. As you are learning the outlines, write each one 3 times.

have each thank-that letter put-please

Phrases. Read and write the following phrases until you can do so without hesitation. In your notetaking, use only those phrases which seem natural to you.

there are there is this is this is not she cannot

NOTES TO READ AND WRITE

Read the following notes until you can read them without hesitation. Then turn to the key and write your own notes from the print. Say each sentence to yourself as you write it. Check your notes with those in the text.

Note that standard abbreviations for months are used in the second and fifth sentences. When you take notes, use the abbreviations that you now use automatically. You will find a list of standard abbreviations in your *Handbook.*

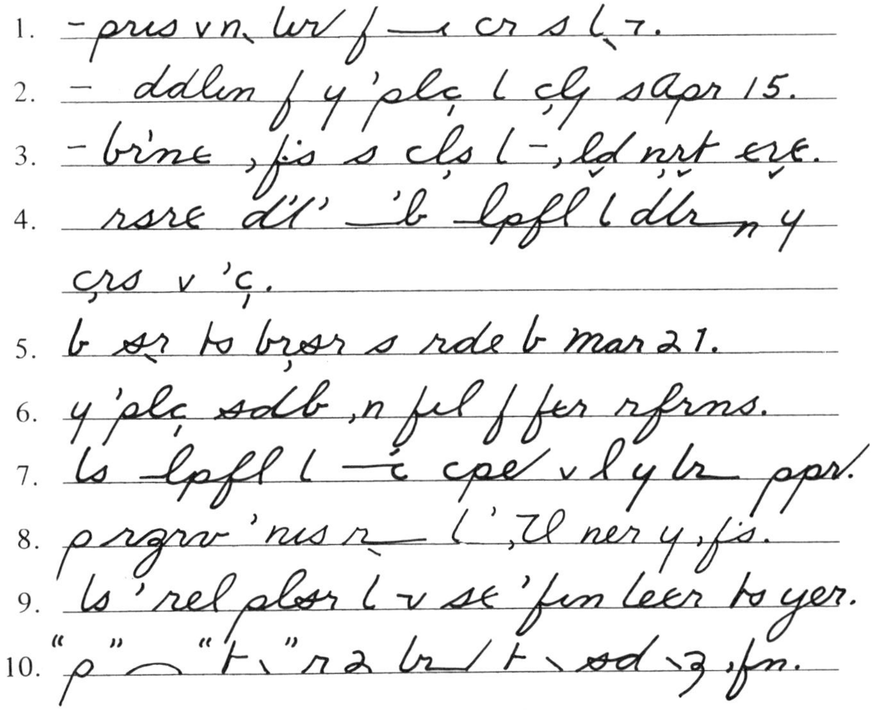

OMITTING VOWEL SYMBOLS

Many writers find they can read their notetaking outlines *in context* without reference to the vowel symbols. If you can read your notes quickly and easily with some vowel symbols omitted, you should leave them out. However, you should *always* write vowels that come first in a word.

In this text and in the *Handbook* you will find that some vowel symbols are omitted from words written in context.

NOTETAKING APPLICATIONS

1. Complete the self-checks in Unit 7 in your *Handbook.*
2. Use Tape 2 Side A from the *Notetaking Tape Library* to build speed. If the tapes are not available, your instructor will read the words and sentences to you while you take notes.
3. If time permits, complete the Optional Applications.

KEY TO *NOTES TO READ AND WRITE*

From this point on, all practice sentences will be marked off in groups of 20 standard words. The number 20 in parentheses after sentence No. 2 below indicates that there are 20 standard words in the first 2 sentences.

1. The price of new tires for my car is too high.
2. The deadline for your application to college is April 15. (20)
3. The branch office is close to the Old North Church.
4. Research data may be helpful to determine your course of action. (40)
5. Be sure this brochure is ready by March 21.
6. Your application should be on file for future reference. (60)
7. It is helpful to make copies of all your term papers.
8. Please reserve a nice room at a hotel near your office. (80)
9. It is a real pleasure to have such a fine teacher this year.
10. "Please" and "thank you" are 2 terms that you should use often. (100)

Chapter 8

A NOTETAKING APPROACH TO LISTENING

You have seen how notetaking can help you absorb more from your reading. Notetaking is even more important in grasping, remembering, and recalling information from lectures and other listening activities. Why are good notes more critical when listening than when reading? When you read, you have complete control over the "instant replay." You can reread a passage as many times as necessary to assure comprehension. But if you miss a lecturer's main point, you have no way to go back and recapture it. Without notes (or a tape recorder), you cannot "relisten" to a lecture.

STUDY-TYPE OF LISTENING

If you are not in the habit of taking class notes, you can probably improve your performance in school dramatically if you begin today to apply the suggestions below.

Analyze and anticipate the content of lectures. You may say, "How can I analyze a lecture *before* it is given?" You will usually have several sources for anticipating the content of an upcoming lecture and for preparing yourself to take good notes.

1. Examine the course outline or syllabus. A topical list of lectures and related readings is your best source of what to expect in lecture courses.
2. Pay careful attention to a lecturer's final statements. A summary statement often ends with a transition to the next lecture. Unfortunately, many students stop listening before a lecturer makes his summary. Here is a typical scene at the close of a class. Lecturer in economics: "Today we have discussed . . ." (Students shut their notebooks, pens are put away, eyes shift to the clock, listening has ceased.) ". . . 3 major causes of inflation. In the next lecture, we will examine 4 ways to control inflation." If you were attentive, you would get 2 cues from the statement. First, you know that your notes for the next lecture will have 4 main headings (4 ways to control inflation), probably with considerable explanation, supporting detail, and examples. Second, you would check today's notes to make sure you have down as main points "3 major causes of inflation." Take a moment to *star* or *underline* these main points in your notes, so that you will pick them up readily as you review.
3. Read your text assignments in anticipation of the next lecture. Reading assignments between lectures will often introduce you to special terms and help you anticipate the content of the next lecture.

Ask yourself questions that you feel will be answered. Consider the example above. You know the next economics lecture will deal with 4 remedies for inflation. What questions might you have in mind as you do your reading before the next lecture? How do the 4 remedies differ? How are they similar? How do economists decide which remedy or remedies to use? How do the various remedies affect the consumer, the businessman, the politician?

Posing questions to yourself will help you not only to become an active listener but also to anticipate possible examination questions. For example, the attentive student in the example above could anticipate exam questions like these: "List 3 major causes of inflation and describe one of the causes in detail." Or perhaps, "Compare and contrast 4 ways to control inflation."

Concentrate on the main ideas. When you listen–just as when you read–the main ideas are what you want. You become an active listener as you ask yourself in the course of a lecture: Is that a main idea? An explanation? An illustration?

Most lecturers habitually use certain words or gestures to emphasize their main points. After you have heard a lecturer 2 or 3 times, you should be able to *predict* when a main point is coming. Some pound the desk. Others use numbers to signal points to remember, "First," "Second," "Another important point," "Finally." Other cues include words expressing superlatives: "The best explanation," "The most significant factors." Sometimes a question will be used to summarize important ideas: "What were Lincoln's major concerns after Gettysburg?" "Why do economists fear inflation?" As you listen for these cues, you become an active listener. Then you will learn more from listening, make better notes, and remember more of what you hear.

Use your notetaking skill to record the main ideas. Summarize the main ideas in your own words as you listen, using as many outlines as you can. Add examples and detail to fix main ideas in your mind.

How much should you write down? No one can tell you precisely. You need enough to remind you of what the lecturer said. You certainly do not need everything the instructor says. On the other hand, single words or phrases that seem like good reminders as you put them down, may let you down when review time comes. As you develop skill in listening and in taking notes, you will discover a happy medium. Until you are sure of yourself, it is better to take down too much than too little. You will find specific suggestions for writing your notes in Chapter 9.

Review your lecture notes promptly. Check your notes for accuracy and completeness while the lecture is still clear in your mind. Add details as they come to mind. Use the left half of the page to add questions and additional points to remember. Underline the main points so you can pick them up readily when you review the notes again.

A 15-minute review of a set of notes within an hour or so of a lecture is often worth twice that amount of study time at a later date. A prompt second exposure (review) will help to make a lasting impression. (Remember the sun tan.) However, if you wait too long to review, the effects of the lecture (the first exposure) will be gone and you have to relearn the entire lecture from your notes.

Another good way to review a lecture is to check your notes with those of another student. Do you both have the same main points?

Select a seat that is free of distractions. As with a concert or the theater, you will get more out of a lecture if you are near the center of action. If you sit in the back, movements of those in front can distract you, and you may have difficulty in hearing. If you are a "window gazer," sit so that you look away from windows when you look at the speaker.

SUMMARY OF STUDY-TYPE OF LISTENING

Study-type of listening is similar to study-type of reading. You set the stage by anticipating what you will be learning. You come to the lecture with questions in mind that you expect to have answered. You listen for main ideas and supporting details, and you use your notetaking skill to record them in your own words. You review your notes promptly.

TO CONSIDER AND DISCUSS

1. Why are good notes more critical when listening than when reading?
2. Explain how you can usually predict when a main point or series of points will come up in a lecture.
3. How much should you write down in notes of a lecture?
4. Why is a prompt review of one's lecture notes more productive than a review at a later date?

WRITING SHORTCUTS

Syllables *In-En-Un*. Write a capital N to express the syllables *in-en-un*.

Cover the printed words and read the notes until you can read them without hesitating. Then cover the outlines and write each word as you read it from print. Check your notes and correct any errors you made. Practice writing the notes until you can read and write them rapidly and accurately.

until   unless   increase   indicate   individual   income

involve   insure   envelope   encourage   indeed   informative

engineer   invite   enable-unable   injury   unknown

Prefix *ad*. Write a capital a to express the prefix *ad*.

As you read each outline, practice writing it several times. Do this for all of the words. When you can write all of the words fluently, cover the print and write each outline only once. Then read your own notes. If you have difficulty reading your notes, rewrite them and read them again.

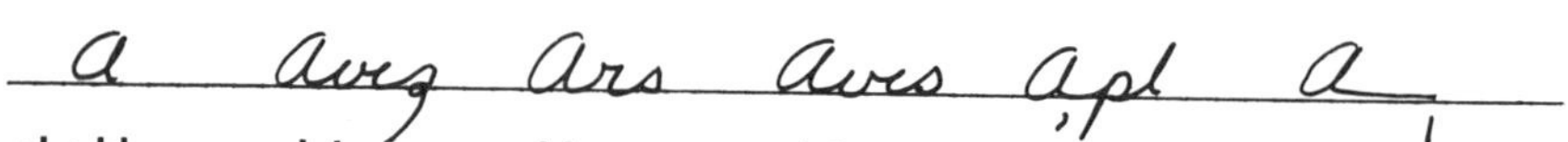

ad-add   advise   address   advice   adopt   admission

Combination *st*. Write a capital S to express the *st* combination.

Cover the print and read the words until you can read them without hesitation. Then increase your writing rate by scribble-writing each of the words 3 times. Remember to keep your eyes on this copy while you are scribble-writing.

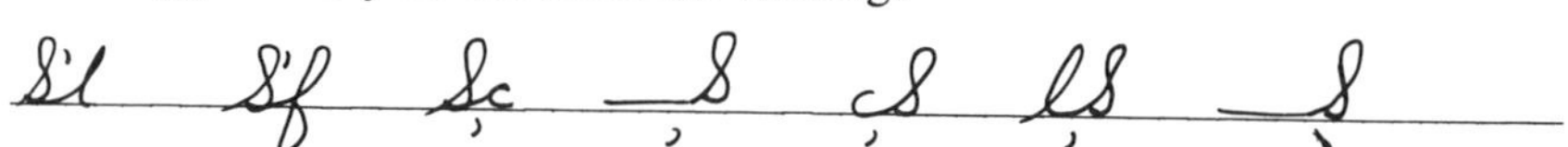

state   staff   stock   most   cost   lost   must

best   just   study   trust   statement   still   past

Ndsre eSt cSm 'gns Sde tS

industry **estate** **customer** **against** **steady** **test**

Abbreviated words. As you study the print and outlines of the new abbreviated words, write each outline until you can do so accurately and without hesitation. Then write each word while it is being dictated to you.

— 's 'bo S bz

am-more **has** **about** **city-street** **business**

NOTES TO READ AND WRITE

Read the following notes until you can read them without hesitation. Then turn to the key and write your own notes from the print. Say each sentence to yourself as you write it. Check your notes with those in the text.

1. -ppr \ pbls 's -ne fin feer Sre.
2. d \ lv n strn sc v ,ld eSt?
3. Nfr , 'bo crer/s 'vlbl n lbrre.
4. sprv, s 'dfclt lsc.
5. \ — 's rcl l-,fs v a_,f 'n cly cllg.
6. Cfun y r 'rc l-sbjct.
7. pln l Nclds_ sol 'clvle/ Ny scjl.
8. -frS -pr \ -c — 'gl \ -jb.
9. nl secrle s' -jr Csrn l l b_/.
10. p ars - Cvn ,n Oct 4.
11. bz _ Ndsre n -jr srs v jb ld'.

12. oS's – ptnsl f rpd grt.
13. –cplet finnsl Stm/ Nbl –Sf l cpr grt rt/.
14. Nvlv e cld N s_ 'clvt.

NOTETAKING APPLICATIONS

1. Complete the self-checks in Unit 8 in your *Handbook.*
2. Use Tape 2 Side B from the *Notetaking Tape Library* to build speed. If the tapes are not available, your instructor will read the words and sentences to you while you take notes.
3. If time permits, complete the Optional Applications.

KEY TO *NOTES TO READ AND WRITE*

1. The paper you publish has many fine feature stories.
2. Do you live in the southern section of the old estate? (20)
3. Information about careers is available in the library.
4. Supervision is a difficult task. (40)
5. You may write to the office of admission for a new college catalog.
6. Confine your remarks to the subject. (60)
7. Plan to include some social activities in your schedule.
8. The first impression you make may get you the job. (80)
9. National security is a major concern at all times.
10. Please address the convention on October 4. (100)
11. Business and industry are major sources of jobs today.
12. Our city has the potential for rapid growth. (120)
13. The complete financial statements enable the staff to compare growth rates.
14. Involve each child in some activity. (140)

Chapter 9

OUTLINING IN NOTETAKING

As you have seen, notetaking is more than simply taking down what someone says or writes. Several skills are required, skills you can develop only with practice. So don't be discouraged if your first notes do not seem to help much in studying and reviewing. Here are some suggestions for writing your notes so that they will be effective learning aids.

USE YOUR WRITING SHORTCUTS

It is important that you force yourself to use the writing shortcuts you are learning so that you use them automatically as you take notes. Without these time-savers, you will spend too much of your time getting down what you hear and read and not enough time on other vital notetaking activities–selecting main ideas, analyzing detail, and summarizing in your own words.

A 2-COLUMN OUTLINING SYSTEM

As suggested earlier, you should write your notes with a ballpoint pen on lined 21.6 by 26.9 cm. (8½ x 11") paper. Write notes only on one side of the paper and plan to use 2 columns, a "record" column and a "recall" column.

The record column. Use the right column to record all input from others. For example, you write lecture notes in the right-hand column, the record column. Similarly, you make reading notes in the right-hand column. You may want to make the right column wider than the left.

The recall column. The left column you save for your own input. Here you write key phrases, summarizing labels, possible exam questions, and the like. Your notes in the recall column should be very brief reminders of what is in the right column. Some of your writing in the left column might be done during a lecture or reading, but most of your notes in the recall column will be added when you review.

THE 2-COLUMN APPROACH IN ACTION

A brief example will show how to use the 2 columns. As you review your notes from a lecture on "Causes of Inflation," you note the following main heading in your record column, "Sharply increased demand for goods and services, a major cause." In your recall column you might write: "Major cause of inflation." Then you read on in the record column and note that you have taken down details and examples to show how the pressures of consumer demand can cause prices to rise as shortages develop. In your recall column you add this question opposite the explanation, "How does increased demand cause inflation?"

Restating major ideas as questions. You will find that most major ideas can be restated in the form of a question–questions you can use to test your own understanding of a lecturer's or writer's main points. If you jot down such questions for all the key ideas in your notes, chances are good that you will find the final exam questions in your recall column!

Reviewing with the recall column. When it is time to review for an examination, remove your notes from your notebook and arrange them in an overlapping fashion so that only the recall column is visible. Then start down the recall columns and answer your questions and respond to your other cues. For example, when you come to the cue, "Major cause of inflation," can you recall what it is without consulting the record column? Can you answer your own question, "How does increased demand cause inflation?" Used in this way, your notes become an efficient system for learning and reviewing.

OUTLINE OR PARAGRAPH FORM?

The form you use for writing down your notes in your record column will depend in part on your own preference and in part on the nature of the material recorded.

Reading notes. You should certainly plan to use the outline form in the record column for most of your reading notes because you usually have headings and subheadings to help you understand the organization of the reading matter. However, you may find the paragraph form better for reading notes in literature, drama, and other courses where you must write down impressions and feelings.

Lecture notes. In taking lecture notes, the skill of the lecturer may dictate the form to use in the record column. Use the outline form with lecturers who organize material logically because the relationship among the various ideas will then be clear in your notes. However, if a lecturer rambles or if the organization is not clear to you, you are probably better off writing your notes in paragraph form.

Geography I

Jan. 21, 19--

Recall	Record
	I. Meteorology s - Sde v ert
define -eterlge ⓐ	'L sfr weather ⌒ cli'l
weather ⓐ cli'l	Cd.
	A. Weather = 'L sfrc Cd
	,n ' givn d'
	B. Climate = 'vrj Cd over
	' period v h
giv 4 cz v	II. Main cz v dfrns n
weather ⌒ dfrns	weather ⌒ cli'l
n cli'l	A. l, ⌒ r pressure ssl
	1. l, pressure 're rzll
(rv - charts ,n	when air warms ,p
pp. 17-18)	⌒ ruz. Example: brpc
	r generally l,
	2. r pressure 're rzll
how dz cl 'r	when cl 'r sinks
'fcl pressure?	Example: plr ryn
	generally r
	B. 'lltd ⌒ lltd
what s - efcl v	1. 'lltd s -l 'bv se
'lltd ,n weather	lvl
⌒ cli'l?	2. lltd s distance
	fr equator
	C. 're v land ⌒ water

EXAMPLE OF A 2-COLUMN OUTLINE

PARAGRAPH FORMAT

As its name implies, the paragraph format calls for a paragraph for each major idea with supporting details in the same paragraph. Of course, numbers may be used in the paragraph to indicate a series of points. An example follows:

PROPERTIES OF HUMAN COMMUNICATION

First consider the language man uses to express his thoughts. There are between 3,000 and 10,000 languages in the world today if you count dialects. Five major languages are Chinese, English, Hindi-Urdu, Spanish, and Russian. More than 2/3 of the world's population speaks one of them. English is most important in printed material . . .

OUTLINE FORMAT

The format of an outline is simple once you have studied it; it's filling in the blanks that becomes a problem. A format showing the relative position of various items is shown below:

HEADING

I. ________ (Main Idea) ________

   A. ________ (Sub Topic) ________

   B. ________ (Sub Topic) ________

      1. ________ (Supporting Material) ________

      2. ________ (Supporting Material ________

         a. ________ (Further Refinement) ________

         b. ________ (Further Refinement) ________

II. ________ (Main Idea) ________

When you use the outline format, keep it as simple as possible. Remember, your outline must be complete enough to remind you of what was said. The example below shows how the outline format reveals the relative importance of the various points.

PROPERTIES OF HUMAN COMMUNICATION

I. The languages man uses to express his thoughts.
   A. There are between 3,000 and 10,000 languages today.
   B. More than 2/3 of the world's population speaks one of the following languages:
      1. Chinese
      2. English
      3. Hindi-Urdu
      4. Spanish
      5. Russian
   C. English the most important in terms of printed material.

RECOPYING NOTES

Unless your notes are practically illegible or poorly organized, it is usually a waste of time to type or recopy notes. All you will learn is how to recopy notes! It is far better to spend your time reciting from the notes you have in your recall column.

Editing and supplementing your notes is a different matter, however. When you review, for example, you may think of points that you want to add to your notes or ideas you may have picked up after the lecture was made. By all means, add such material either in the record or recall columns.

TO CONSIDER AND DISCUSS

1. Explain why it is important to reduce to a minimum the time you take to write your notes.
2. In a 2-column system for taking notes, explain how you can use the recall column to review for an examination.
3. How can a lecturer's skill affect the form you use for taking notes?

WRITING SHORTCUTS

Expressing the past tense. Make a small dash under the last letter or symbol in an outline to show that *d* or *ed* is added to a root word.

Cover the print of each line of words and read the notes until you can read them as fast as you can read the print. Then write each outline several times to build speed.

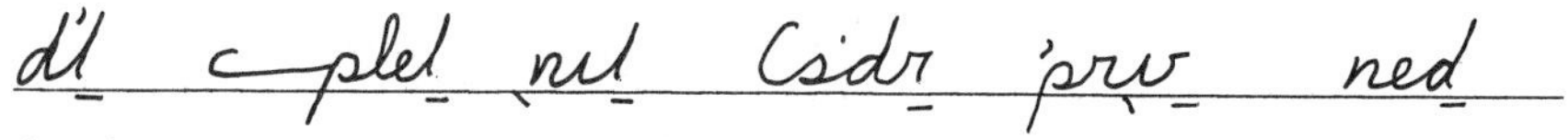

dated **completed** **united** **considered** **approved** **needed**

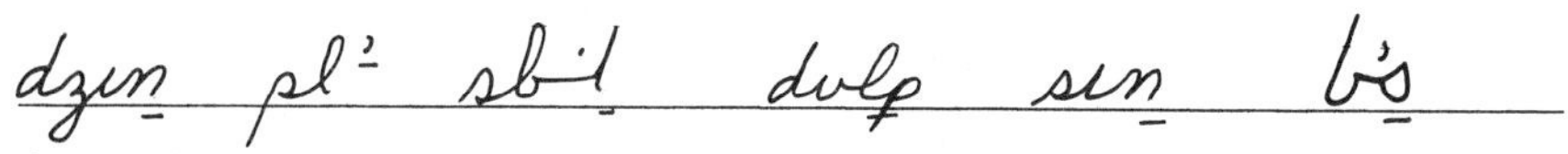

designed **played** **submitted** **developed** **signed** **based**

limited **concerned** **continued**

NOTES TO READ AND WRITE

Read the following notes until you can read them without hesitation. Then turn to the key and write your own notes from the print. Say each sentence to yourself as you write it. Check your notes with those in the text.

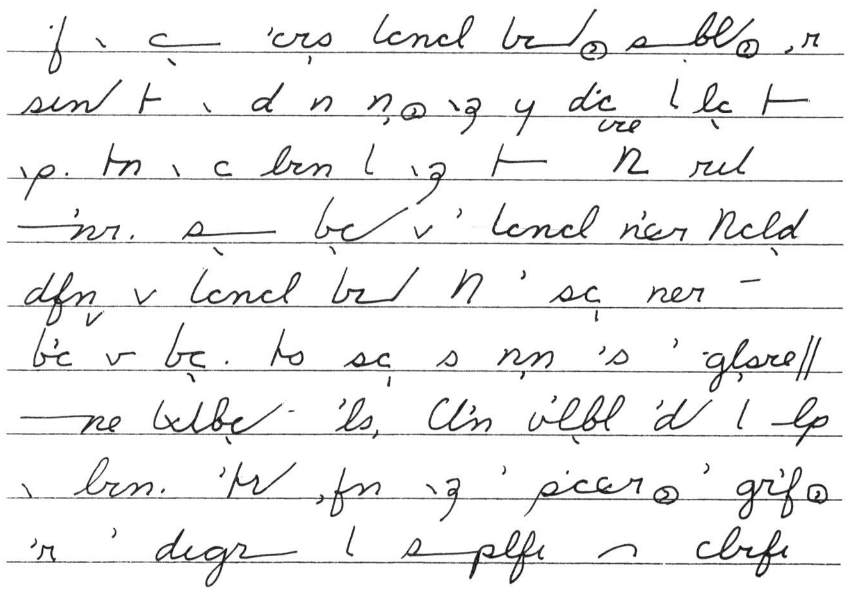

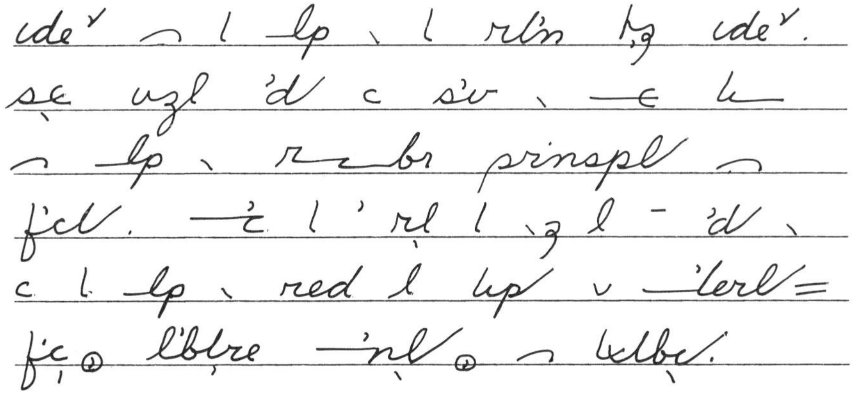

PUNCTUATION–PARENTHETICAL EXPRESSIONS

This is the first of a number of punctuation reviews that deals with errors college students make frequently in their written assignments and examinations. To give you practice in applying the specific rules, each punctuation rule has one or more self-checks in your *Handbook*. If you need additional practice and guidance in punctuation, refer to "A Writer's Guide to Punctuation and Style" in the back of your *Handbook*.

A parenthetical expression may be a single word, or a group of words. You can identify parenthetical expressions because they may be omitted from a sentence without changing the meaning of the sentence.

Rule for parenthetical expressions. Place a comma before and after all parenthetical words, or group of words.

Examples. The sentences that follow include parenthetical words and groups of words. Note how each parenthetical expression is preceded and followed by commas. You can omit the word or words between the commas in each sentence without changing the meaning of the sentence.

1. We will, however, spend the summer at the seashore.
2. Over half of the class, on the other hand, was absent on Tuesday.
3. Amy and Shawn were elected president and vice president, respectively, of the student council.
4. The United States and Canada, which have been settled by many nationalities, have developed multicultural societies.
5. Our instructor, who wears flamboyant ties, is an excellent public speaker.

SPELLING PRACTICE

Check the spelling of each of the following words. They are among those most frequently misspelled by college freshmen. After you have studied the spelling of these words, write the outline for each word on a separate piece of paper. Then close your text and write out each word from the outline you have written. Check your spelling with the list in the text and review the words you misspelled.

accommodate	divine	medicine
across	effect	morale
all right	embarrass	necessary
almost	environment	noticeable
among	familiar	occurred

KEY TO *NOTES TO READ AND WRITE*

If you come across technical terms, symbols, or signs that you do not know, use your dictionary to look them up. Then you can learn to use them in the right manner. Some books of a technical nature include definitions of technical terms in a section near the back of the book. This section is known as a glossary.

Many textbooks also contain valuable aids to help you learn. Authors often use a picture, a graph, or a diagram to simplify and clarify ideas and to help you to retain those ideas. Such visual aids can save you much time and help you remember principles and facts. Make it a rule to use all the aids you can to help you read all types of materials–fiction, laboratory manuals, and textbooks.

NOTETAKING APPLICATIONS

1. Complete the self-checks in Unit 9 in your *Handbook*.
2. Use Tape 2 Side B from the *Notetaking Tape Library* to build speed. If the tapes are not available, your instructor will read the words and sentences to you while you take notes.
3. If time permits, complete the Optional Applications.

EXAMINATION 1

All the examinations are in the back of your *Handbook*. Each is to be removed along the perforation. When directed to do so by your instructor, remove and take Examination 1. This test covers the material that has been covered up to this point in your text and *Handbook*.

Chapter 10

OBSERVING AND NOTETAKING

Psychology professor: "Now as I place the rats in the maze a second time, *observe* their reaction to . . ."

Ecology professor: "Your report on this field trip should include your *observations* of . . ."

Marketing professor: "Remember, next week your report is due on your *observations* of customer impulse buying . . ."

Yes, much of your future academic and professional work will call for skill in observing and recording what you have seen. Specific suggestions for building your observing and recording skills are given below.

Use appropriate materials. In some situations where you must take notes as you observe, a loose-leaf notebook will be too cumbersome. You should plan to use smaller bound notebooks with wide lines for taking notes on field trips, in laboratories, and in other situations.

Be prepared mentally. When you are to observe, advance preparation is important so that you can focus your attention on details. Before a sportswriter enters the pressbox to report on a ball game, he tries to anticipate critical situations he will observe. Will Jones break his slump? Can the Braves keep their winning streak alive? How will this blazing hot sun affect play?

Before a detective reaches the scene of a crime, he reviews all the information he already has about the crime, the victim, the possible motives. This preparation sets the stage for his search for clues, interrogation of suspects, and other observations.

Similarly, you should prepare yourself for observing. Lecture notes or your reading should alert you to the important details to look for in observing class demonstrations and experiments.

Keep the main idea in mind. Every experiment in chemistry class, every demonstration in the physics lab, and every geology field trip has a main idea or purpose. What principle is being demonstrated? What should the end product be? Write down the purpose, and keep that purpose in mind as you watch or participate. What does the instructor expect you to learn? Answers to these questions will help you direct your attention to matters of importance. Then as you record the details of what you see, the relationships among the various details should become clear.

Study laboratory manuals. When you have a specific laboratory activity assigned, take a few minutes to study your laboratory manual before the lab period. Then you can anticipate what you are to look for at various points in the experiment.

TO CONSIDER AND DISCUSS

1. Several professions might be called "observing" professions because they require skill in observing. Name at least 2 observing professions and be prepared to tell why you classify them as such.
2. You have been selected to help report on the local radio the play-by-play action of your school football team. Be prepared to tell how you might prepare for that assignment.

WRITING SHORTCUTS

Sounds of *w-wh.* Write a long, upward, slanted, straight line for the sounds of *w* and *wh.* Begin the stroke below the line so the next letter rests on the line.

Cover the print and read the outlines until you can read them as fast as you can read the print. Then write each of the outlines and read them back. If any of your outlines are difficult to read, practice them until you can read and write them easily.

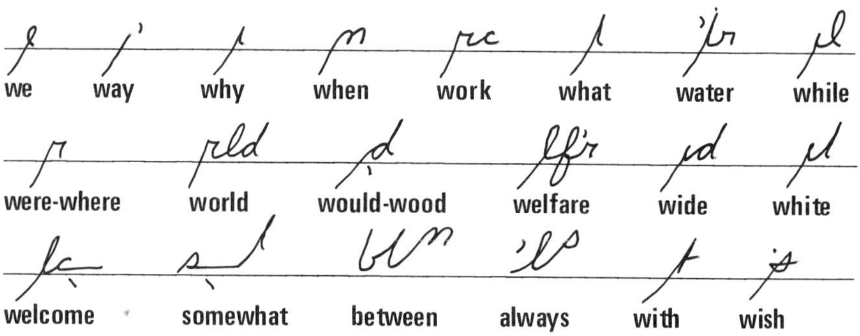

Syllable *an.* Write a small a for the syllable *an.*

As you read each word, write the note for each word several times. Then write the note for each word once and read your own notes back.

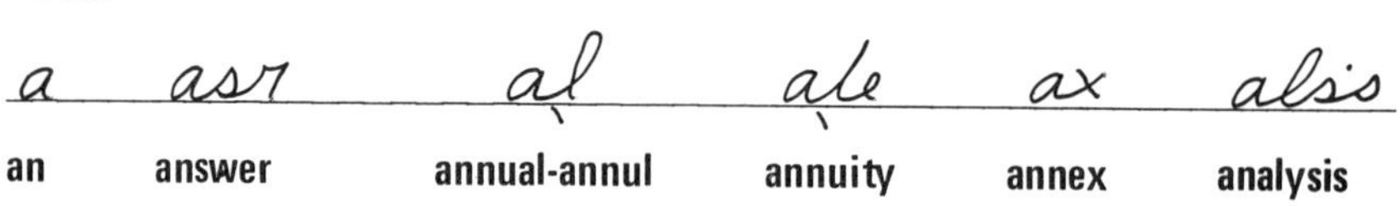

Syllables *dis-des*. Write a capital  for syllables *dis* and *des*. Some writers prefer to use this form  .

Read the following words until you can read them fluently. Then increase your writing rate on these words by scribble-writing each word 3 times.

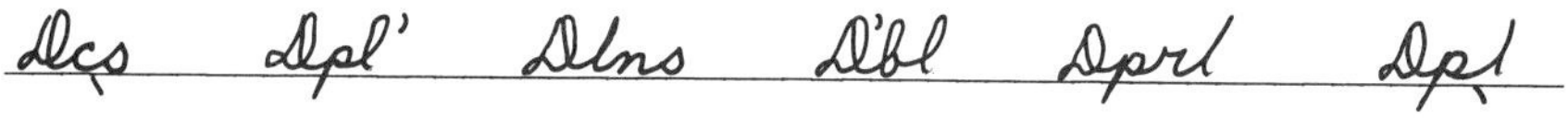

discuss **display** **distance** **disable** **desperate** **dispute**

Abbreviated words and phrases. Memorize the following abbreviated words so that you can write them automatically. Write each of the abbreviated words and phrases until you can do so rapidly and accurately.

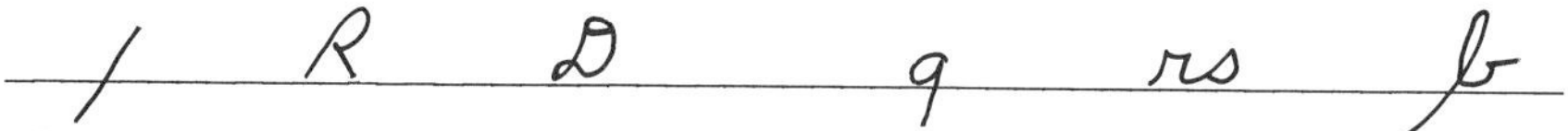

will-well **order** **department** **go-good** **receive** **will be**

will not **we are** **we can** **we have**

NOTES TO READ AND WRITE

Read the following notes until you can read them without hesitation. Then turn to the key and write your own notes from the print. Say each sentence to yourself as you write it. Check your notes with those in the text.

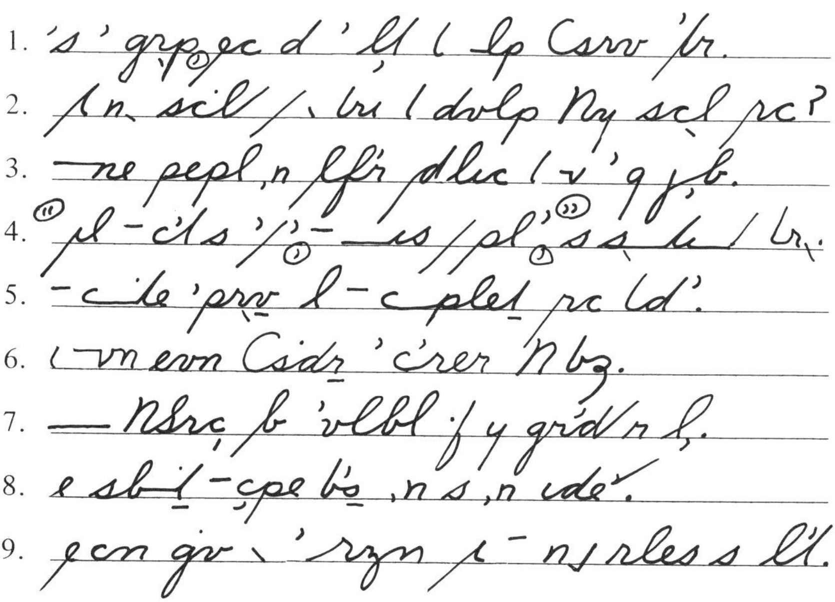

10.
11.
12.
13.
14.

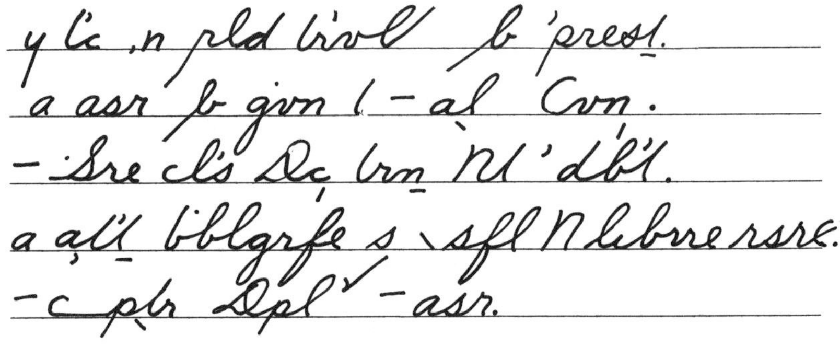

NOTETAKING APPLICATIONS

1. Complete the self-checks in Unit 10 in your *Handbook.*

2. Use Tape 3 Side A from the *Notetaking Tape Library* to build speed. If the tapes are not available, your instructor will read the words and sentences to you while you take notes.

3. If time permits, complete the Optional Applications.

KEY TO *NOTES TO READ AND WRITE*

1. As a group, we can do a lot to help conserve water.
2. What new skills will you try to develop in your school work? (20)
3. Many people on welfare would like to have a good job.
4. "While the cat is away, the mice will play," is sometimes true. (40)
5. The committee approved all the completed work today.
6. I have not even considered a career in business . (60)
7. More instruction will be available if your grades are low.
8. He submitted the copy based on his own ideas. (80)
9. We cannot give you a reason why the news release is late.
10. Your talk on world travels will be appreciated. (100)
11. An answer will be given at the annual convention.
12. The history class discussion turned into a debate. (120)
13. An annotated bibliography is useful in library research.
14. The computer displays the answer. (140)

Chapter 11

NOTETAKING AND LETTER WRITING

"But what will I say in the letter?"

If that question troubles you when you have a letter to write, maybe your notetaking skill can make the job easier.

Plan what to say. An important first step is to jot down all the points you want to cover. Don't worry about how you will word your letter at this point. Simply put down the facts that you must give.

Arrange your facts in a logical order. Once you have all the facts down, number them in what you feel would be a logical order. Now, using your numbered list of facts as an outline, your letter will practically write itself.

An example. Less than 2 months ago, you bought a tape deck for your car from Modern Stereo, Inc. A week later, the tape deck failed to work. Modern Stereo repaired it free of charge. The unit has just failed again and Stereo says it cannot be repaired. You get no satisfaction when you ask for a new unit or for your money back. You call the Consumer Protection Agency and talk to Ms. Frances Taylor. She suggests you put your complaint in writing and that you send the sales slip with the letter.

Below you will see the list of facts you have jotted down using your notetaking skill. Then the facts are numbered in the order you think will be most logical. The actual letter you write is Letter 1 in the "Style Manual" in your *Handbook*. Note how the numbered facts have been followed in writing the letter.

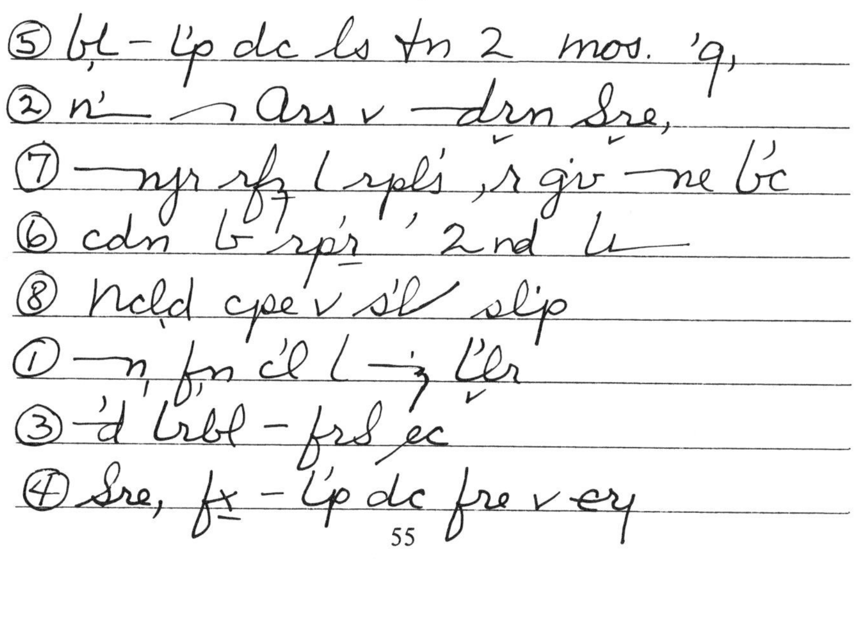

TO CONSIDER AND DISCUSS

Assume that you are vice-president of the Student Council with special responsibility for programs. The Council decides to sponsor a series of talks on career opportunities. People from local businesses and professions will be invited to speak. It is your responsibility to write letters inviting these speakers. Using your notetaking skill, jot down the points you would want to cover in your letter. Then number the points in the order you think they should come in the letter.

WRITING SHORTCUTS

Combinations *ing-ng-thing*. Write a long curved stroke ‿ to express *ing, thing,* and the *ng* sound in words like *think.*

Cover the print and read the words until you can read them without hesitation. Then write each of the outlines 3 times rapidly and accurately.

planning building meeting during covering

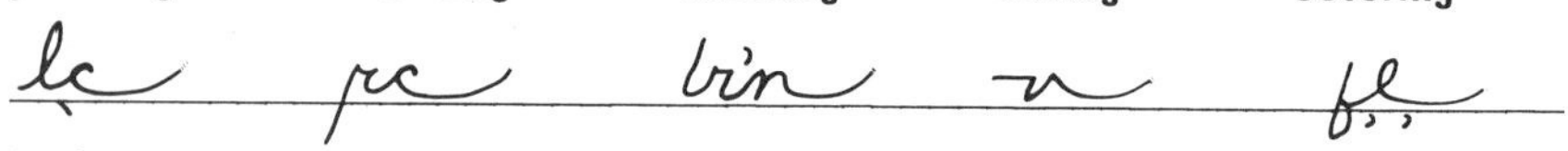

looking working training having following

answering making being bring long

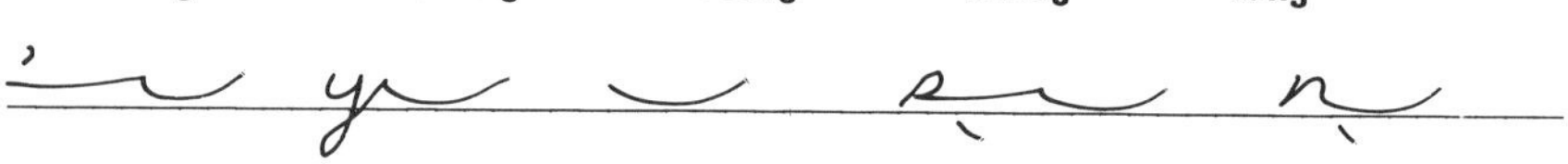

among young thing something nothing

think bank pink frank drank drink

Endings in *ly*. Make a short dash close to the word to add *ly* endings. Write the final *l* in words that end in *l* and then add the dash for *ly.*

When you can read the first line fluently, cover the print and write the outlines. Practice until you can write each word rapidly and accurately. Follow the same procedure for each line.

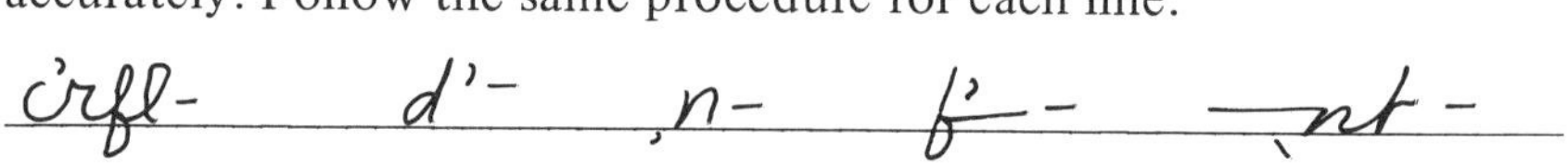

carefully daily only family monthly

possibly highly usually easily actually

really assembly normally earliest

Abbreviated words and phrases. The following commonly-used words must be memorized to help you build your notetaking speed. Read the notes until you can read them as fast as you can read the print. Then practice writing them until you can write them fluently and accurately.

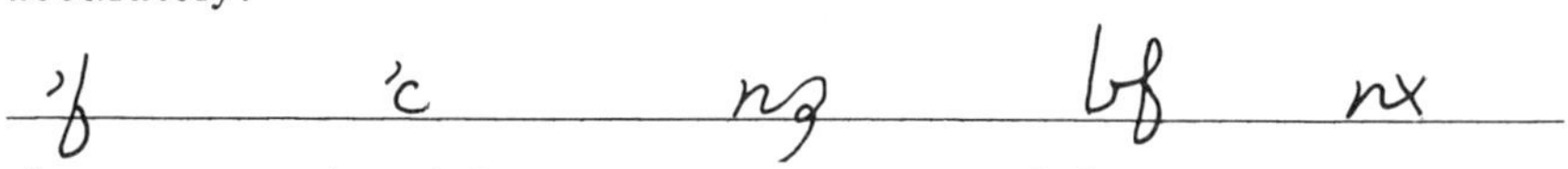

after acknowledge necessary before next

to see I am to type to study to read

NOTES TO READ AND WRITE

Read the following notes until you can read them without hesitation. Then turn to the key and write your own notes from the print. Say each sentence to yourself as you write it. Check your notes with those in the text.

1. 
2. 
3. 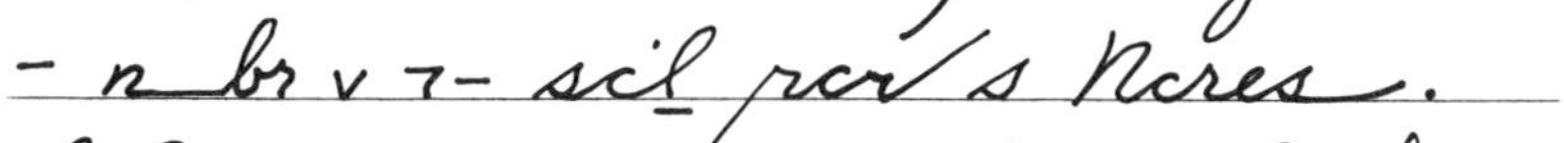
4. 
5. 
6. 
7. 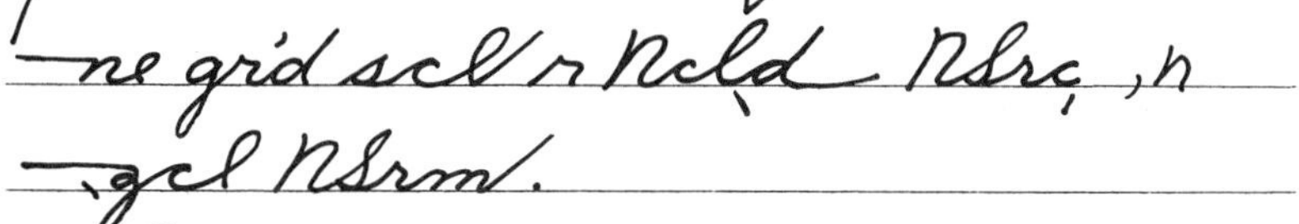
8. 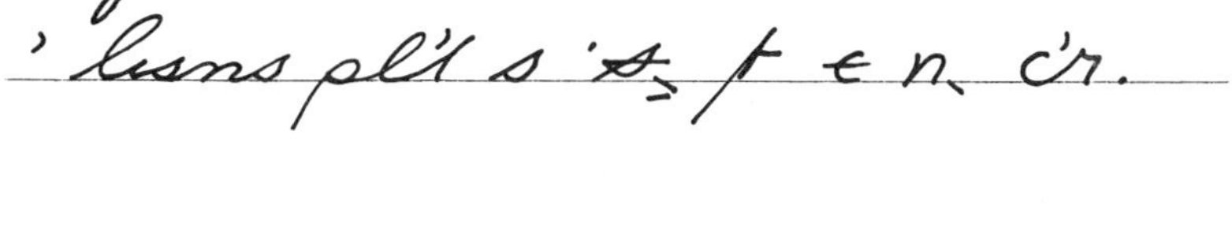

9. 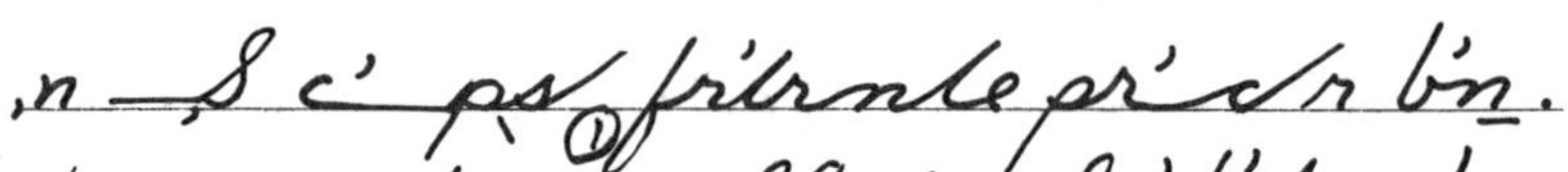

10. 

11. 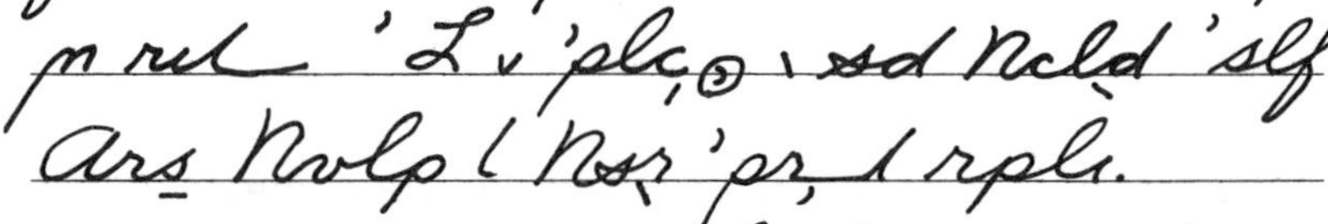

12. 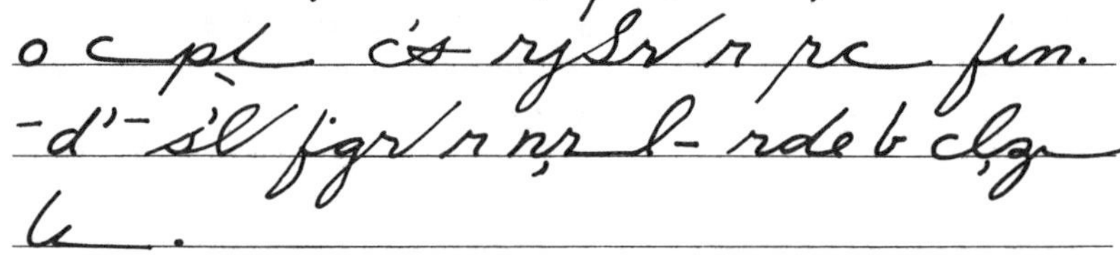

NOTETAKING APPLICATIONS

1. Complete the self-checks in Unit 11 in your *Handbook.*
2. Use Tape 3 Side A from the *Notetaking Tape Library* to build speed. If the tapes are not available, your instructor will read the words and sentences to you while you take notes.
3. If time permits, complete the Optional Applications.

KEY TO *NOTES TO READ AND WRITE*

1. The results of the tests were conclusive.
2. The study committee received the necessary data yesterday. (20)
3. The number of highly skilled workers is increasing.
4. All discontinued courses are listed with the counselors. (40)
5. Athletic competition is open to both men and women.
6. Please acknowledge receipt of all contributions. (60)
7. Many grade schools are including instruction on musical instruments.
8. A license plate is issued with each new car. (80)
9. On most campuses, fraternity pranks are banned.
10. Frankly, too much publicity can be a bad situation. (100)
11. When writing a letter of application, you should include a self-addressed envelope to insure a prompt reply. (120)
12. Our computing cash registers are working fine. The daily sales figures are normally ready by closing time. (140)

Chapter 12

PLANNING A RESEARCH PAPER

Why are writing skills so important for the first-year college student? Because professors in large freshman classes frequently judge their students' knowledge and progress by the quality of their written work. In large classes, there is seldom an opportunity for students to reveal their understanding of what has been taught through recitation and discussion. It's the written word that counts.

This chapter and the 5 chapters that follow offer suggestions for improving your writing skills. These chapters take you step-by-step through the process of writing a research or term paper. Included is help on picking a topic, planning your research, using the library, preparing footnotes, writing your first draft, and proofreading your final draft.

THINK POSITIVELY

Don't despair if you are afflicted with a paralysis of the pen when you are faced with a writing assignment. Even experienced writers sometimes have difficulty getting started.

As with most creative work, writing requires positive thoughts. When a paper is assigned, don't say to yourself, "I can't possibly write about that." Instead, you should accentuate the positive by jotting down all the questions you can think of about a topic.

For example, if you were asked to write a paper on advertising for a class in Consumerism, you should begin immediately by writing down all the questions that occur to you about advertising. Ask questions that relate to you, your interests, and your experiences. In only a few minutes, you might end up with questions such as the following:

How does advertising affect me? My family?

How does advertising influence my classmates' purchases?

Which TV commercials do I remember? Why?

Who are the major advertisers in the community?

To help stimulate more questions and ideas, you should do some background reading to become better acquainted with your subject.

GATHER BACKGROUND INFORMATION

An encyclopedia article is often the best place to start your background reading about a topic. As you read to get an overview of your subject, jot down additional ideas and questions that the article suggests to you.

For example, if you read an encyclopedia article on "Advertising," you might add these questions to those you wrote down earlier:

What are the advantages of the different forms of advertising (TV, newspaper, billboard, etc.)?

How do companies decide which forms of advertising to use? How much to spend?

What are the job prospects in the advertising business?

What do people in the advertising business actually do?

What are some laws that govern advertising?

With this expanded list of questions, the next step is easy. You then make a list of possible topics based on the questions that appeal to you most. At this point, don't ask yourself, "What will I say?" All you are trying to do is to get a list of possible topics to investigate. Here are some specific topics that are suggested by the questions above:

The Influence of Advertising on My Family's Purchases
The Advantages and Disadvantages of Advertising on TV
Major National Laws that Control Advertising
Career Opportunities in Advertising
A Survey of the Major Advertisers in Our Community

How do you decide which one to pursue?

PICKING A TOPIC

When you are faced with selecting a specific topic, ask yourself the following questions about your tentative choice. If you can answer "yes" to all the questions, your choice is probably a good one.

1. Do I want to find out more about the subject? If you do, your interest in the subject will make it easier to write about.
2. Do I know something about the topic? Advance knowledge of possible sources of information can certainly make a writing job easier. Look to your own experience for ideas.
3. Can I find out more about the topic in the library, from other sources, or from interviews with others? If you cannot easily find several good sources of information about a topic, pick another subject.
4. Can I limit the topic so that I can complete it in the time available to me? Be realistic about the time that you think will be required. Avoid that night-before-the-paper-is-due agony that comes when you discover too late that a topic is too broad for you to cover.

When you have selected a topic that fits the above questions, then you are ready to begin to plan your investigation (research). You will find suggestions for making research plans in the next chapter.

SUMMARY

Good writing skills are especially important for college freshmen, and these skills can be developed with practice. Therefore, every writing assignment is an opportunity for you to try out and perfect various techniques for improving your writing skill. Plan to use these specific suggestions for getting started with your next writing assignment:

1. Start by asking yourself questions about your topic. As you jot them down, you will drive away self-doubts and set your mind to work.
2. Do some background reading about the topic to add more questions and ideas to your list.
3. As you look over your list of questions, specific topics will occur to you. Write them down.
4. From among the possible topics, select one that interests you, that you can explore further with available resources, and that you can narrow down to manageable size.

TO CONSIDER AND DISCUSS

1. In a social studies class, you are studying conservation of resources. You are assigned a paper on water pollution. Using your notetaking, jot down at least 5 questions that occur to you as you think about the topic. Be prepared to read your questions in class.
2. Try to recall the last paper you wrote. Did you have difficulty getting started? Which of the suggestions in this chapter would have been most helpful to you? Why?

WRITING SHORTCUTS

Combinations of *nt-nd*. Write a curved stroke thus  to express the combinations *nt* and *nd.*

Practice reading the following notes. When you can read them as fast as you can read the print, cover the outlines and write the notes from the print. If your outlines are difficult to read, rewrite them and read them again.

find kind land end recent want

current second plant entire attend hand

send-sent | center | mind | event | recommend

Combination *sp*. Write a small printed *s* to express *sp*.

As you read each outline below, write it 3 times. When you have practiced all the words, you should be able to read and write them rapidly and accurately.

speed | speaker | speak | space | spent-spend

spending | specific | correspond | grasp | inspection

Abbreviated words and phrases. Memorize the following abbreviated words so that when you hear them you can write them automatically. Then write the words and phrases until you can do so rapidly and accurately.

important-ance | great | question | satisfy-factory

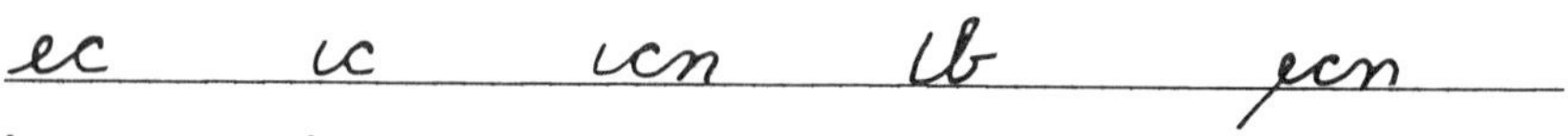

he can | I can | I cannot | to be | we cannot

NOTES TO READ AND WRITE

Read the following notes until you can read them without hesitation. Then turn to the key and write your own notes from the print. Say each sentence to yourself as you write it. Check your notes with those in the text.

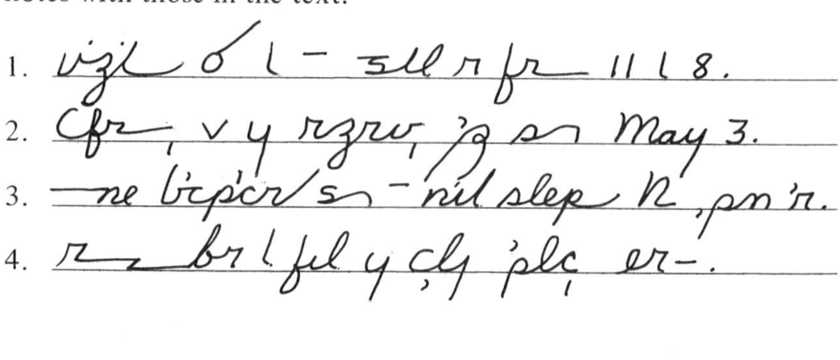

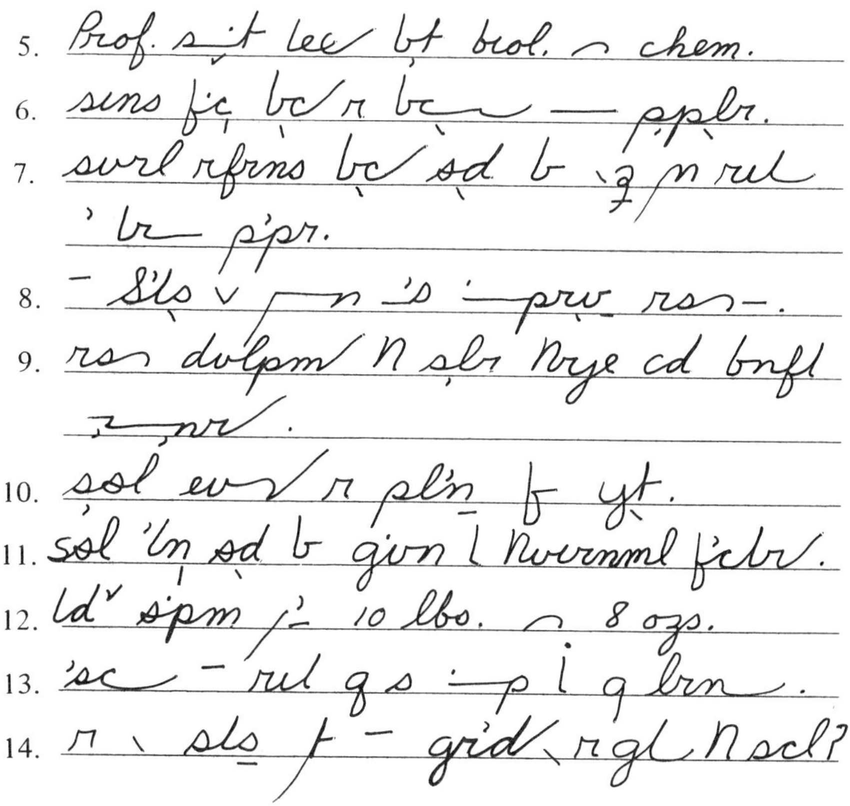

SPELLING PRACTICE

Check the spelling of each of the following words. They are among those most frequently misspelled by college freshmen. After you have studied the spelling of these words, write the outline for each word on a separate piece of paper. Then close your text and write out each word from the outline you have written. Check your spelling with the list in the text and review the words you misspelled.

analyze	fascinate	parallel
apparent	February	privilege
appearance	finally	receive
argument	friend	recommend

NOTETAKING APPLICATIONS

1. Complete the self-checks in Unit 12 in your *Handbook*.

2. Use Tape 3 Side B from the *Notetaking Tape Library* to build speed. If the tapes are not available, your instructor will read the words and sentences to you while you take notes.

3. If time permits, complete the Optional Applications.

KEY TO *NOTES TO READ AND WRITE*

1. Visiting hours at the hospital are from 11:00 to 8:00.
2. Confirmation of your reservation was sent May 3. (20)
3. Many backpackers spend the night sleeping in the open air.
4. Remember to file your college application early. (40)
5. Professor Smith teaches both biology and chemistry.
6. Science-fiction books are becoming more popular. (60)
7. Several reference books should be used when writing a term paper.
8. The status of women has improved recently. (80)
9. Recent developments in solar energy could benefit homeowners.
10. Social events are planned for the youth. (100)
11. Special attention should be given to environmental factors.
12. Today's shipment weighed 10 pounds and 8 ounces. (120)
13. Asking the right question is important to good learning.
14. Are you satisfied with the grades you are getting in school? (140)

Chapter 13

THE PRELIMINARY OUTLINE

In the last chapter, you learned ways to stimulate your thinking and narrow your ideas down to a specific topic. Once you have picked a topic, you should begin work on your preliminary outline.

FOCUS ON YOUR READER

Now you must shift your attention from *your* topic and *your* interests to the interests of your prospective readers. Unless you know something about your audience—whether it be your instructor, fellow students, or someone else—you are not likely to communicate effectively. Here again, your ability to ask the right questions is important.

Your preliminary outline should be a list of questions that your reader is likely to ask. How can you put yourself in your reader's shoes? A good technique is to pretend you are telling a classmate what you discover or learn. If, for example, you were to tell a classmate the topic you have picked, the first question might be, "Why did you pick that topic?"

Your reader is not likely to be satisfied if you simply say that your topic is "interesting" or "important." You must tell why the topic is interesting or important to you and your reader. The answers to these "why important" questions are often the first few paragraphs of a research paper.

What does your reader already know about your topic? Answers to this question will suggest how much background information you must provide. What other questions will arise in your reader's mind? Jot down the questions you feel you will have to answer and then list them in logical order. If you can find a patient listener at this point, read the proposed title of your paper and your questions. You will probably get some good suggestions.

A 2-COLUMN OUTLINE

Many experienced writers combine their preliminary outline with a tentative plan for finding answers to their questions. In the left column, they list all the questions that a reader might ask or need information about. They leave space under each question so that other questions may be added later. Then in the right column, they indicate possible sources to consult for answers to the questions. The example that follows shows the use of a 2-column outline.

PRELIMINARY OUTLINE FOR
CAREER OPPORTUNITIES IN ADVERTISING

Reader Questions	*Sources and Ideas*
1. Why is the topic important?	To help me choose a career. I like work on a school newspaper. A classmate's father works for an ad agency, and his job sounds interesting. Check books and articles on the impact of advertising.
2. What is the future of the advertising business?	Check growth. In almanacs? Recent magazine articles? Are there advertising organizations? Yearbooks?
3. What are the job specialties in advertising? What is done in each?	Book on advertising business? Check with guidance office? Examine a college text on advertising.
4. In which specialties are there shortages of people?	Guidance office? Check on government estimates of manpower needs. Is there an employment agency in town that specializes in jobs in advertising? If so, try to get an interview?
5. What aptitudes are required?	Books on advertising business. Guidance office materials.
6. What preparation is recommended?	Books or articles on advertising business. Check catalogs of colleges that offer programs in advertising. Interview neighbor who is in advertising.
7. What are salaries and other benefits in advertising?	Books on advertising.
8. What are the negative aspects of an advertising career?	Job security? Books on advertising. Magazine ads.

ADVANTAGES OF THE 2-COLUMN OUTLINE

Combining your list of questions with a tentative plan for finding answers results in the following advantages:

1. The questions serve as reminders of precisely what you need from the library, from a survey, from an interview, or from other sources. With this plan, you avoid the aimless searching that wastes so much time.
2. The outline breaks up the research and writing tasks into small pieces that you can work on one at a time.

3. The 2-column format enables you to plan your research priorities. You can work at once on those questions for which sources are on hand and put off other questions until resources are available.
4. This form of outline can easily be converted into a topic or sentence outline if your instructor prefers this kind of working outline.

TO CONSIDER AND DISCUSS

1. Explain what is involved when you "... put yourself in your reader's shoes."
2. Which feature of the 2-column preliminary outline do you feel will be most helpful to you? Explain why.

NOTES TO READ AND WRITE

Read the following notes until you can read them without hesitation. Then turn to the key and write your own notes from the print. Say each sentence to yourself as you write it. Check your notes with those in the text.

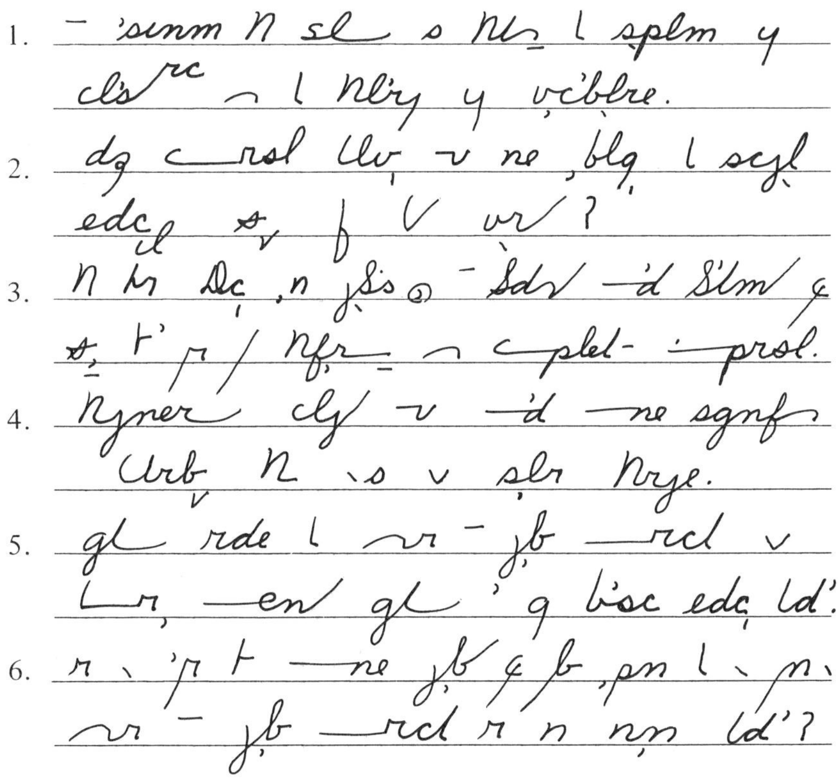

7. 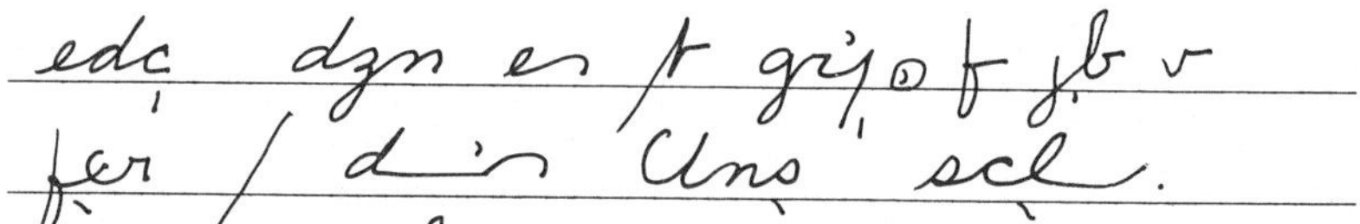

8. 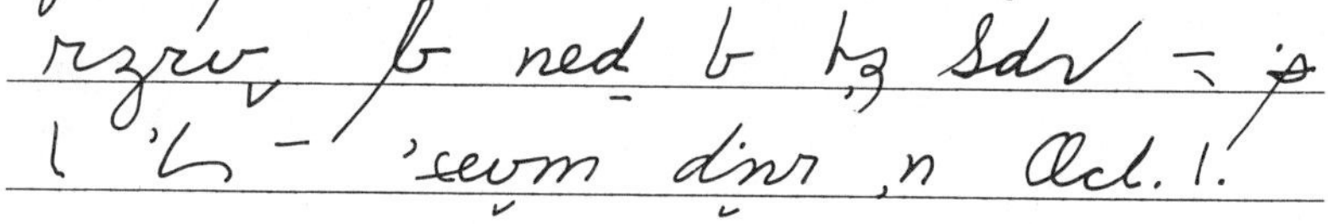

PUNCTUATION REVIEW–CONTRACTIONS

A contraction is a shortened form of a word (can't for cannot) or a group of words (we've for we have). Contractions are useful to inject an informal tone in your writing. You should not use them, however, if you seek a formal style.

Rule for contractions. Use an apostrophe to mark the omission of a letter or letters in contracted words.

Examples. The sentences below include contracted words. Note how the apostrophe shows that letters have been omitted. The words that have been contracted are given at the end of each sentence.

1. We've decided we can't join you at the camp site. (we have, cannot)
2. They've talked with all who are going and report that everybody's planning to bring lunch. (they have, everybody is)
3. Don't worry if you've forgotten your lunch, there's an excellent restaurant near the ball park. (do not, you have, there is)
4. I haven't seen the new model yet, but I'm sure it will be an improvement over the old one. (have not, I am)
5. It's extremely important to follow the instructions. (it is)
6. He was graduated with the Class of '77. (1977)
7. Since it's been winning, the fṛeshman team has improved its record. (it has)

Special caution. Note that Sentence 7 includes *it's* (with an apostrophe) and its (without an apostrophe). How can you tell when to use the apostrophe? Apply this test: If you can substitute *it is* or *it has* for *its,* you insert the apostrophe; otherwise, you omit it. Try this test on Sentence 7. You can substitute *it has* for *it's*, but the sentence makes no sense if you try to substitute *it is* or *it has* for *its record.* When in doubt, always apply this test to find out whether or not to insert an apostrophe in *its.*

SPELLING PRACTICE

Check the spelling of each of the following words. They are among those most frequently misspelled by college freshmen. After you have studied the spelling of these words, write the outline for each word on a separate piece of paper. Then close your text and write out each word from the outline you have written. Check your spelling with the list in the text and review the words you misspelled.

believe	generally	safety
benefit	government	schedule
benefited	governor	separate
business	heroes	shining
choose	incidentally	similar

NOTETAKING APPLICATIONS

1. Complete the self-checks in Unit 13 in your *Handbook.*
2. Use Tape 3 Side B from the *Notetaking Tape Library* to build speed. If the tapes are not available, your instructor will read the words and sentences to you while you take notes.
3. If time permits, complete the Optional Applications.

KEY TO *NOTES TO READ AND WRITE*

1. The assignment in spelling is intended to supplement your class work and to enlarge your vocabulary. (20)
2. Does commercial television have any obligation to schedule educational shows for its viewers? (40)
3. In their discussion on justice, the students made statements which showed they were well informed and completely impartial. (60)
4. Engineering colleges have made many significant contributions in the use of solar energy. (80)
5. Getting ready to enter the job market of tomorrow means getting a good basic education today. (100)
6. Are you aware that many jobs which will be open to you when you enter the job market are not known today? (120)
7. Education does not end with graduation; for the job of the future will demand continuous schooling. (140)
8. Reservations will be needed by those students who wish to attend the Achievement Dinner on October 1. (160)

Chapter 14

DEVELOPING YOUR LIBRARY SKILLS

If you have examined a college catalog recently, you may have noticed a strong emphasis on independent study. You will find that many institutions encourage or require students to undertake special-interest projects or independent research studies. Almost without exception, these programs call for heavy use of libraries. This chapter gives practical suggestions for building your library skills.

SECTIONS OF THE LIBRARY

When you enter a library where you plan to work, your first step should be to familiarize yourself with the various sections where materials are stored. Most libraries have the following sections:

Catalog section. The library catalog is actually a huge card file. Here is where you look to find out if a library has a specific book and how many books it has on a given subject. The library card catalog also gives the location of every item in a library. In large libraries, the catalog files may occupy an entire room.

Reference section. Here you will find books and other items that give you quick access to specific facts. Included are encyclopedias, almanacs, indexes, atlases, yearbooks, directories, and other resources. You will also find books to help you locate information in other books, magazines, and government documents. Reference books are available to all library users. Usually, they do not circulate (they may not be taken from the room).

Periodical section. In this section or room are magazines, and other materials that are published periodically. In most libraries, recent issues of magazines are kept in open racks. Older issues are usually bound, and may be on open shelves or available only through an attendant. These may also be on microfilm or microfiche.

Reserve section. Materials in this section or room are reserved for certain users. For example, an instructor assigning reading from a book to a large class can request that the book be "put on reserve." The time that each user may have a reserved book is strictly limited. Therefore, more library users may have access to a book that is in the reserve section.

SEARCHING FOR INFORMATION

When you need a person's telephone number, you know from experience to use a telephone book. But what do you do when there is no obvious source that will yield the information you need? For example, answers to questions such as these would require an organized search: Who won the women's 100 meter dash in the 1924 Olympic Games? Is the population of beef cattle declining in Iowa? What will be the estimated energy requirements in the United States 10 years from now? Where is Tasmania, and what are its chief exports?

When you do not know where to find a specific fact or information about a topic, the following sequence is recommended:

General reference books. Try these first. They include encyclopedias and almanacs. Even if they do not give you the specific facts you need, they often suggest sources that will.

Reference books on specific subjects. If you cannot find what you want in a general reference book, then search for a reference book that deals with your specific topic or question. In large libraries you will find hundreds of reference books to help find specialized information. For example, you would consult *Book Review Digest* to find reviews of a specific literary work. For information about a living celebrity, you would look in *Who's Who.* For facts about various aspects of life in the United States, you would consult *Statistical Abstract of the United States.* You should not hesitate to ask a librarian for help in finding the reference books that will be most useful to you.

Standard works. If you cannot find the information you need in reference books, you should then look up a book on your topic in the library catalog. A general book on a given topic by a recognized authority is known as a standard work. You will find such books in the library catalog under the appropriate subject heading. Suggestions for searching for standard works are in the following section on the library catalog.

Periodicals. For up-to-date information about a topic, you should consult magazines. The *Reader's Guide to Periodical Literature* will help you to find what you want in a wide assortment of popular magazines. For current information in special fields, survey the magazines and journals in that field.

USING THE LIBRARY CATALOG

The library catalog usually includes at least 3 cards for each book, an *author* card, a *title* card, and one or more *subject* cards. Each type of card has a special purpose in finding what you want. In most libraries, all cards in the catalog are filed in alphabetical order according to the information on the top line of the card.

The author card. This card gives the most complete information about a book. Therefore, if you know the name of the author of a book you are searching for, always look first for the author card. Author cards are filed last name first, as in a telephone book.

The title card. If you know the title of a book but not the author's name, then look for the title card. These cards are in alphabetical order by title, but the initial words, *A, An,* and *The* are disregarded in filing. For example, the title card for *The Rise of Capitalism* would be filed under *R.*

The subject card. Here is where you look to find all the books a library has about a given subject. For example, in most libraries you would find a subject card for *The Rise of Capitalism* in the C's behind the card headed, *Capitalism.* Books dealing with more than one subject will have a card for each subject. For example, this text would be listed under two subjects, *Notetaking* and *Study Skills.*

When considering a topic to work on, you should check your topic against the proper subject headings in the subject file to make sure that you will have sufficient sources to do a creditable job. If you find many cards on the subject you have selected, a quick look through the subject cards may suggest how you can narrow your topic.

TO CONSIDER AND DISCUSS

1. Assume that you are to write a term paper on a topic that you have not studied before and that you know little about. Be prepared to tell what library resources you would consult and the order in which you would consult them.
2. Try to recall the procedure you used the last time you had to look up information in the library for a term paper or for some other purpose. Write down how your procedures would differ as a result of the suggestions in this chapter.

WRITING SHORTCUTS

Prefixes *fer-for-fore-fur.* Write a disjoined *f* for words beginning with the syllables *fer-for-fore-fur.*

Cover the print and read the outlines until you can read them as fast as you can read the print. Then write each of the outlines once and read them back. If any of your outlines are difficult to read, rewrite them until you can read and write them easily.

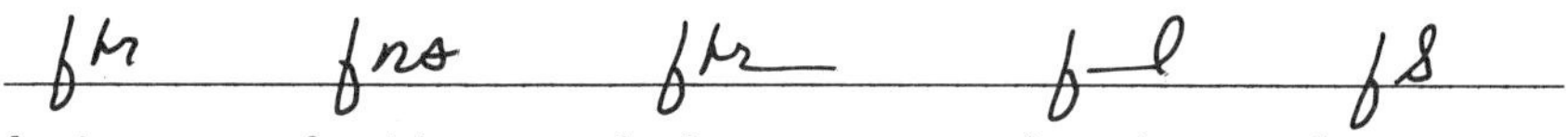

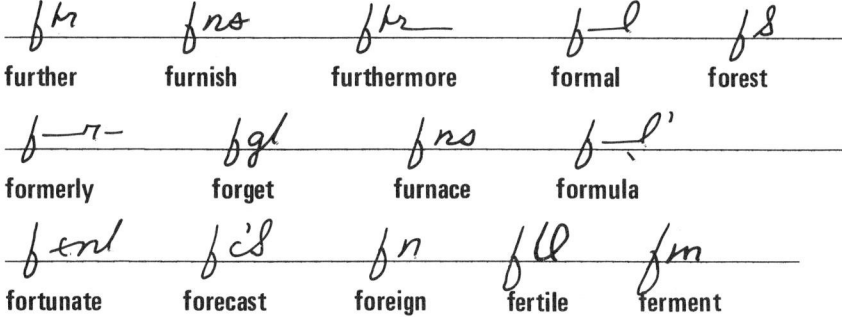

further furnish furthermore formal forest

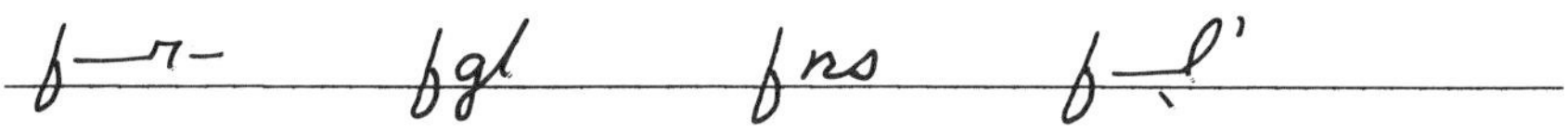

formerly forget furnace formula

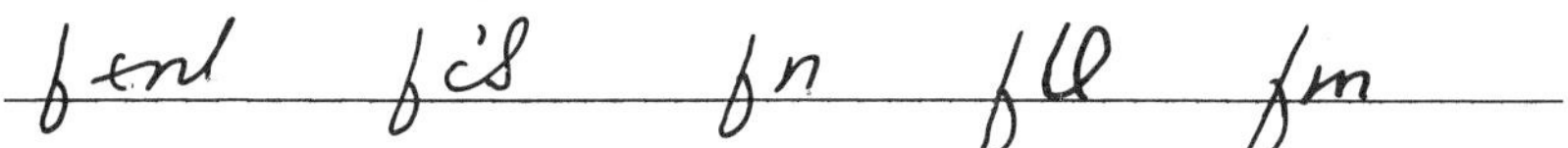

fortunate forecast foreign fertile ferment

Prefixes *pr-vowel* or *p-vowel-r.* Write a disjoined *p* for words that begin with the syllables *pr-vowel* or *p-vowel-r.*

As you read each outline, practice writing it several times. When you can write all of the words fluently, cover the outlines and write each word once from the print. Try to read your own notes.

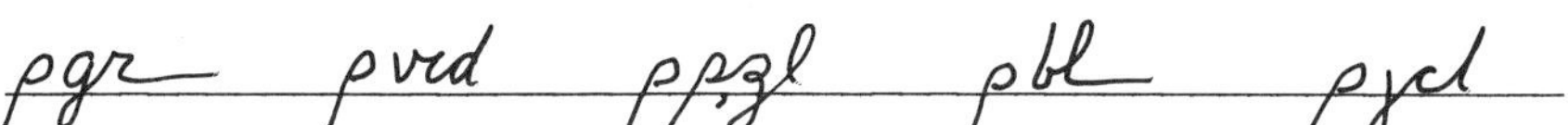

program provide proposal problem project

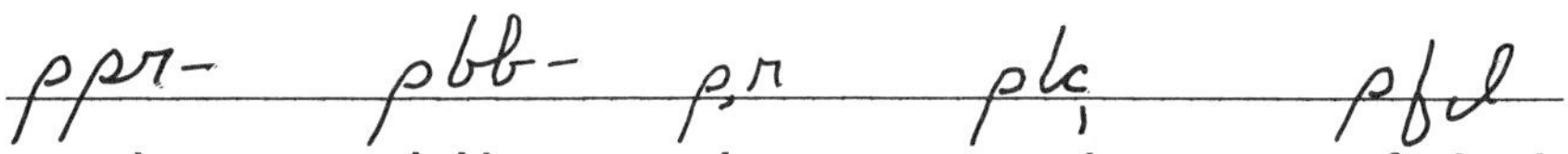

properly probably prior protection professional

perhaps person present prepared purchase

purpose proper progress

NOTES TO READ AND WRITE

Read the following notes until you can read them without hesitation. Then turn to the key and write your own notes from the print. Say each sentence to yourself as you write it. Check your notes with those in the text.

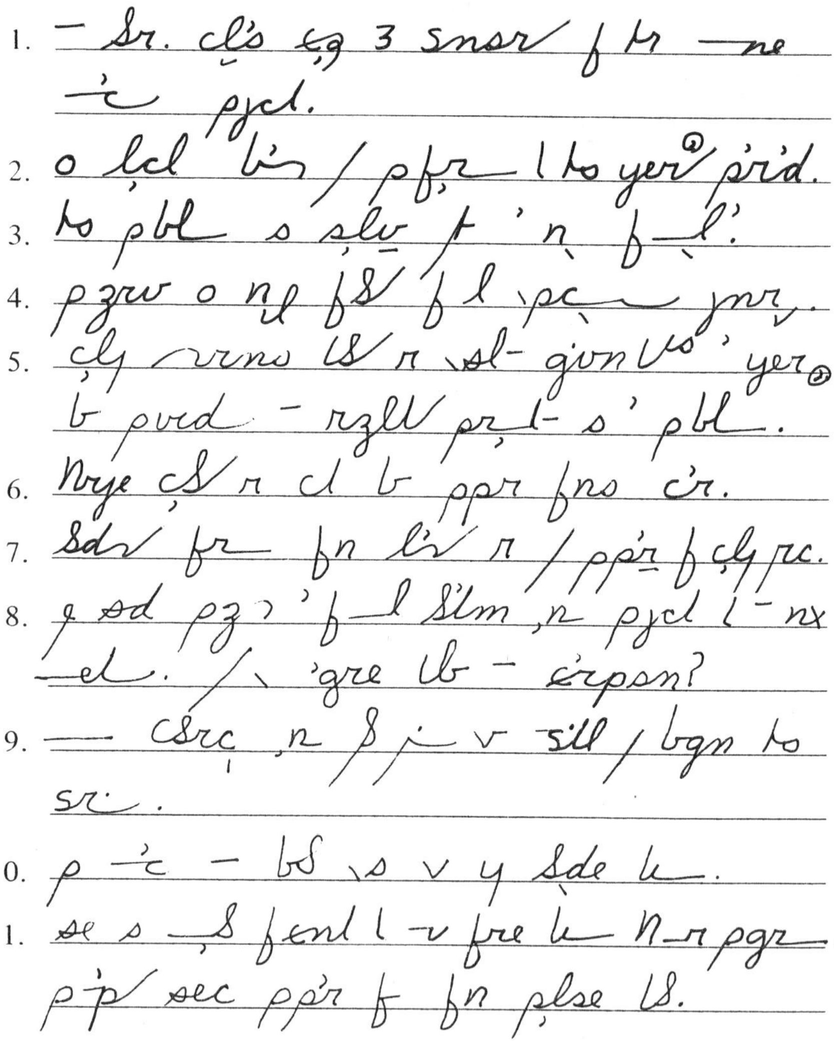

SPELLING PRACTICE

Check the spelling of each of the following words. They are among those most frequently misspelled by college freshmen. After you have studied the spelling of these words, write the outline for each word on a separate piece of paper. Then close your text and write out each word from the outline you have written. Check your spelling with the list in the text and review the words you misspelled.

absence	disease	mathematics
coming	intelligence	studying
committee	its	there
conscientious	judgment	until

NOTETAKING APPLICATIONS

1. Complete the self-checks in Unit 14 in your *Handbook.*
2. Use Tape 4 Side A from the *Notetaking Tape Library* to build speed. If the tapes are not available, your instructor will read the words and sentences to you while you take notes.
3. If time permits, complete the Optional Applications.

KEY TO *NOTES TO READ AND WRITE*

1. The Senior Class chose 3 sponsors for their money-making project.
2. Our local band will perform at this year's parade. (20)
3. This problem is solved with a new formula.
4. Preserve our national forests for all upcoming generations. (40)
5. College entrance tests are usually given twice a year, but providing the results promptly is a problem. (60)
6. Energy costs are cut by proper furnace care.
7. Students from foreign lands are well prepared for college work. (80)
8. We should present a formal statement on the project at the next meeting. Will you agree to be the chairperson? (100)
9. More construction on the west wing of the hospital will begin this spring.
10. Please make the best use of your study time. (120)
11. She is most fortunate to have free time in her program. Perhaps she can prepare for the foreign policy test. (140)

Chapter 15

PREPARING BIBLIOGRAPHIES

A *bibliography* is a list of books, magazines, and other sources that an author has consulted in writing a research paper, an article, or a book. In any research paper you write, you should include in your bibliography all the items you have examined. You need not have read a book or an article to include it in your bibliography. The bibliography is usually the last item in a research paper. You will find an example of a bibliography page in "A Writer's Guide to Format" in your *Handbook*. Examples of bibliographic entries for many kinds of sources are given in your *Handbook* in "A Writer's Guide to Bibliography and Footnotes."

MAKING BIBLIOGRAPHY CARDS

If you have prepared a 2-column preliminary outline as suggested in Chapter 13, the second column suggests sources to consult. Your next step is to compile a card file of specific books, magazine articles, and other sources that relate to your topic. Remember, a good starting place is an encyclopedia article. But don't overlook the other sources suggested in Chapter 14.

Items in the card. Using cards (either small or larger sizes), make a card for each item you find that deals with the topic you have chosen. A bibliography card for a book includes the following items:

1. Author's or authors' full names (last name first).
2. Complete title of the book.
3. Publication facts.
4. Copyright date.
5. Library call number.

In your search for references, you will often run across an item for which you have only part of the information needed to complete the bibliography card. In such cases, fill in as much information as you can and leave blank lines for missing information. Then you can complete the card if and when you consult the actual item.

Accuracy important. It is important that all facts about your sources be recorded accurately on your bibliography cards because these cards will be the source for your bibliography and footnotes. You may use your notetaking outlines in preparing these cards, but write out all proper names.

Bibliography cards from library catalog. You will probably make most of your bibliography cards from the information in the library catalog. To see how to use the library catalog for this purpose, look at the illustrations of a catalog card and the corresponding bibliography card on the next page.

EXAMPLES OF BIBLIOGRAPHY CARDS

The examples below show appropriate entries for bibliography cards for different kinds of sources. Note that all words in book titles and in names of newspapers and magazines are underlined. Articles from magazines or newspapers are put in quotation marks. The call numbers have not been included at the bottom of the card. You would add the call numbers when you consult the library catalog.

Book–one author.

Johnson, Richard T.
A Harvest of Scorn.
New York: Random House,
1956.

Book–with subtitle. Note that the subtitle is also underlined.

Seymour, Harold J.
Designs for Fund Raising: Principles, Patterns, Techniques.
New York: McGraw-Hill Book Company,
1966.

Book–more than 2 authors, second edition. Note that *2nd edition* is not underlined.

Franklin, Robert L., and others.
Anthology of Modern Literature, 2nd edition.
Boston: Little, Brown and Company,
1970.

Book, pamphlet, or monograph–authored by an organization.

None (on author line to indicate no individual author).
Report of the Commission on the Arts.
Washington, D.C.: American Council on Education,
1977.

Magazine article–author named. Note that page numbers are given.

Taylor, Roger G.
"The Modern Novel,"
College English.
December 1976,
pp. 24-29.

Magazine article or newspaper article—author not named.

None (on author line to indicate none given).
<u>Newsweek.</u>
4 June 1976,
p. 16.

SB438 Cactus
L287

Lamb, Edgar.
Popular exotic cacti in color / Edgar and Brian Lamb. — New York : Collier Books, c1975.
176 p. : ill. ; 20 cm.
Includes index.
ISBN 0-02-063340-8

1. Cactus. 2. Cactus—Pictorial works. 3. Succulent plants. 4. Succulent plants—Pictorial works. I. Lamb, Brian Michael, joint author. II. Title.

SB438.L287 1975 635.9'33'47 75-43810
MARC

Library of Congress 75

SAMPLE ITEM FROM LIBRARY CATALOG

Lamb, Edgar, & Lamb, Brian.
Popular Exotic Cacti In Color.
New York: Collier Books,
1975.

SB438 L287

SAMPLE BIBLIOGRAPHY CARD

TO CONSIDER AND DISCUSS

1. How does a bibliography help a reader to judge the quality of a research paper or a book?
2. What items should appear on a bibliography card for a book, and in what order should the items appear?

WRITING SHORTCUTS

Combination *qu*. Write only *q* for the combination *qu*.

Read the notes below until you can read them fluently. Then cover the notes and write the outline for each word accurately and rapidly.

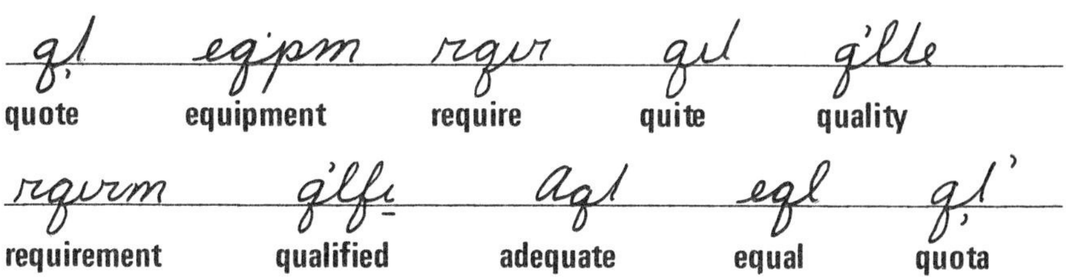

Combination *rd-rt*. Write a capital *R* to express *rt* or *rd* when no vowel occurs between the 2 consonants.

Cover the printed words and read the notes until you can read them without hesitating. Cover each word and write the outline 3 times. Then write each word only once and try to read it back. Are your notes readable? If not, rewrite the outlines until you can read and write all of them easily.

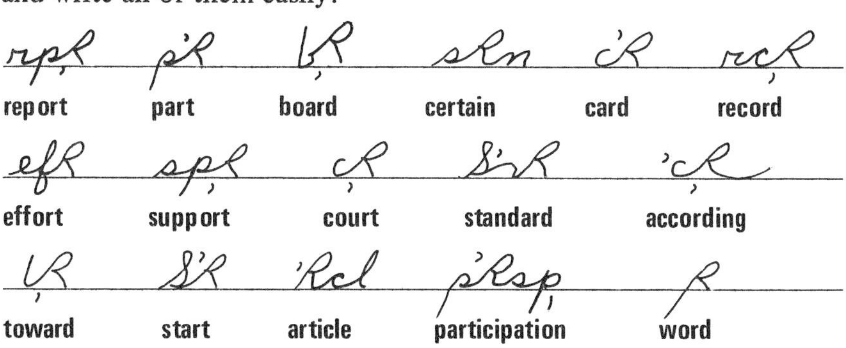

Prefix *under*. Write a small longhand *u* for the prefix *under*.

As you read each outline, practice writing it several times. Do this for all the words. When you can write all of the words fluently, cover the outlines and write each word as you read from the print. Read your notes and rewrite any you cannot read easily.

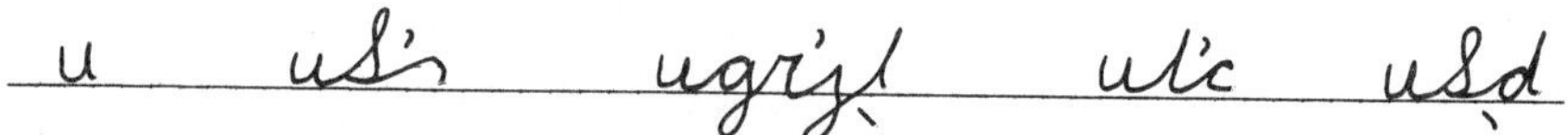

under **understand** **undergraduate** **undertake** **understood**

NOTES TO READ AND WRITE

Read the following notes until you can read them without hesitation. Then turn to the key and write your own notes from the print. Say each sentence to yourself as you write it. Check your notes with those in the text.

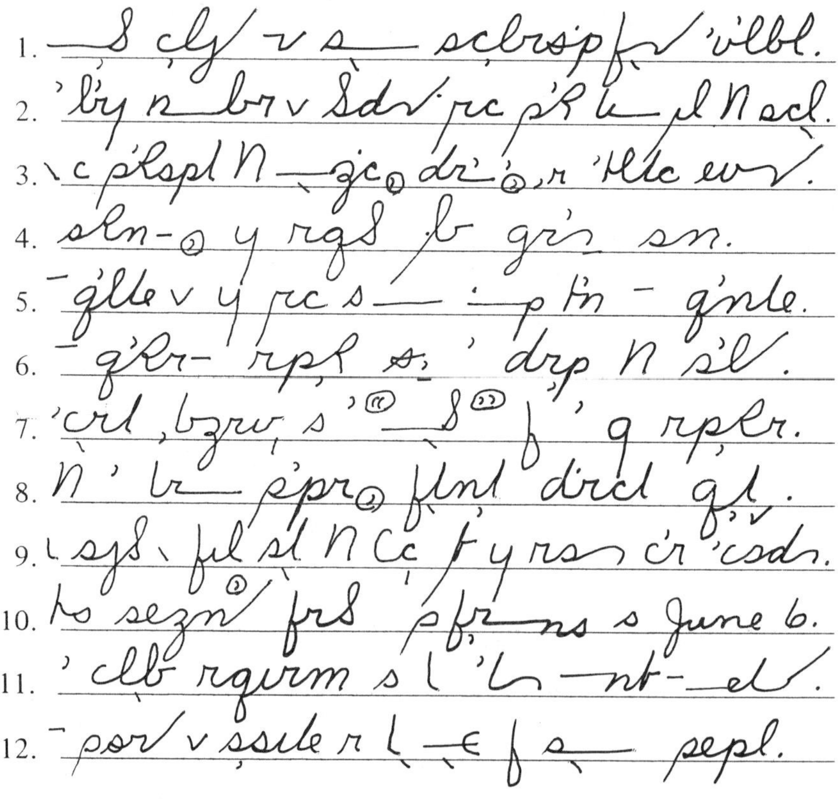

13.

14.

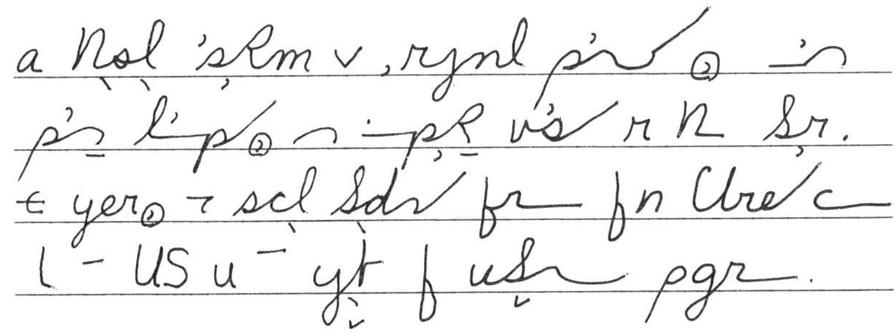

PUNCTUATION REVIEW–QUOTATION MARKS

In most term papers, you will want to quote various authorities to support your ideas. It is important, therefore, that you know how to punctuate quotations.

Rules for punctuating direct quotations. Quotation marks are used to enclose material quoted either from printed matter or speech. The end quotation mark is always placed outside of commas and periods. If a quotation consists of more than one sentence, quotation marks are placed at the beginning and end of the entire quotation. If a quotation consists of more than one paragraph, quotation marks should be placed at the beginning of each paragraph and at the end of the last paragraph only.

Examples. The comments following each sentence call attention to specific rules for placing quotation marks:

1. "Follow the instructions in the manual," said the instructor. (Comma inside the quotation marks.)
2. "Have you seen a good movie lately?" asked Scott. (Question mark inside the quotation marks.)
3. Carol said, "I am going to Hawaii for the first week of my vacation. Then I plan to tour California." (Comma precedes the quotation marks; period inside the quotation marks; entire quotation is in quotation marks.)
4. Did the Senator say, "I will support that bill"? (Question mark outside the quotation marks because the whole sentence is a question.)
5. The officer said, "I heard the witness say, 'Don't move or I'll shoot,' and then I heard 2 shots." (A single quote mark is used to indicate a quote within a quote.)

Rules for punctuating certain titles and special terms. Titles of articles, songs, and radio and television programs should be enclosed in quotations. Special terms and slang expressions are also put in quotation marks.

Examples. The comments following the sentences give specific instructions.

1. My favorite song is "Stardust." (Song titles are enclosed in quotation marks; the end quotation mark is placed outside of period.)
2. If you think your father is "square," you should meet mine sometime. (The slang expression is enclosed in quotation marks; the end mark comes after the comma.)
3. He called himself "emperor," but he was really a dictator. (Special terms are enclosed in quotation marks.)
4. Yesterday's television schedule included a debate on "Meet the Press." (Titles of TV programs are enclosed in quotation marks.)

NOTETAKING APPLICATIONS

1. Complete the self-checks in Unit 15 in your *Handbook*.
2. Use Tape 4 Side A from the *Notetaking Tape Library* to build speed. If the tapes are not available, your instructor will read the words and sentences to you while you take notes.
3. If time permits, complete the Optional Applications.

SPELLING PRACTICE

Check the spelling of each of the following words. They are among those most frequently misspelled by college freshmen. After you have studied the spelling of these words, write the outline for each word on a separate piece of paper. Then close your text and write out each word from the outline you have written. Check your spelling with the list in the text and review the words you misspelled.

controlled	knowledge	villain
definite	laid	weather
despair	library	whether

KEY TO *NOTES TO READ AND WRITE*

1. Most colleges have some scholarship funds available.
2. A large number of students work part time while in school. (20)
3. You can participate in music, drama, or athletic events.
4. Certainly, your request will be granted soon. (40)
5. The quality of your work is more important than the quantity.
6. The quarterly report showed a drop in sales. (60)
7. Accurate observation is a "must" for a good reporter.
8. In a term paper, footnote direct quotations. (80)
9. I suggest you file suit in connection with your recent car accident.
10. This season's first performance is June 6. (100)
11. A club requirement is to attend monthly meetings.
12. The pressures of society are too much for some people. (120)
13. An unusual assortment of original paintings, hand painted lamps, and imported vases are in the store. (140)
14. Each year, high school students from foreign countries come to the United States under the Youth for Understanding program. (160)

Chapter 16

MAKING NOTE CARDS

With your preliminary outline and your bibliography cards before you, you are ready to begin your reading. The importance of this research reading and notetaking cannot be overemphasized. If your bibliography includes sources that are relevant to your topic and if you take good reading notes, your research paper should be relatively easy to organize and write.

A look at your bibliography cards will suggest the best source with which to begin your reading. You should usually start with a source that deals in a general way with your topic, leaving for later any materials on special aspects of your topic.

HOW MANY NOTES?

How many notes should you take? You can spend too much time making reading notes if you fail to keep the purpose of your reading in sharp focus. But most beginning writers err on the side of too few notes. When they begin to write, they find they need more notes to support their ideas. Here are some suggestions for deciding how many notes to take:

1. Take more notes than you can use. The more notes you have on various topics in your outline, the more selective you can be in establishing facts and supporting your ideas.
2. Use more than one source. If you use only one or 2 sources, you may be unable to give proper perspective to your presentation.
3. Strive for balance. If you find many good sources about a particular point, you may end up with far too many notes on that point and too few notes on other points that are equally important.

REASONS FOR MAKING NOTES ON CARDS

The order in which you take your notes will be different from the order in which you use them in your paper. Furthermore, until you finish your reading and begin to write, you will not know which notes you will finally use and which will prove useless. Therefore, you must make your notes so that you can (1) easily add new notes as you find them, (2) rearrange the notes you have in any order that seems best, and (3) put aside those notes that you decide not to use. For these reasons, you should make your reading notes on cards and use a separate card for each note. The cards should be the same size as your bibliography cards.

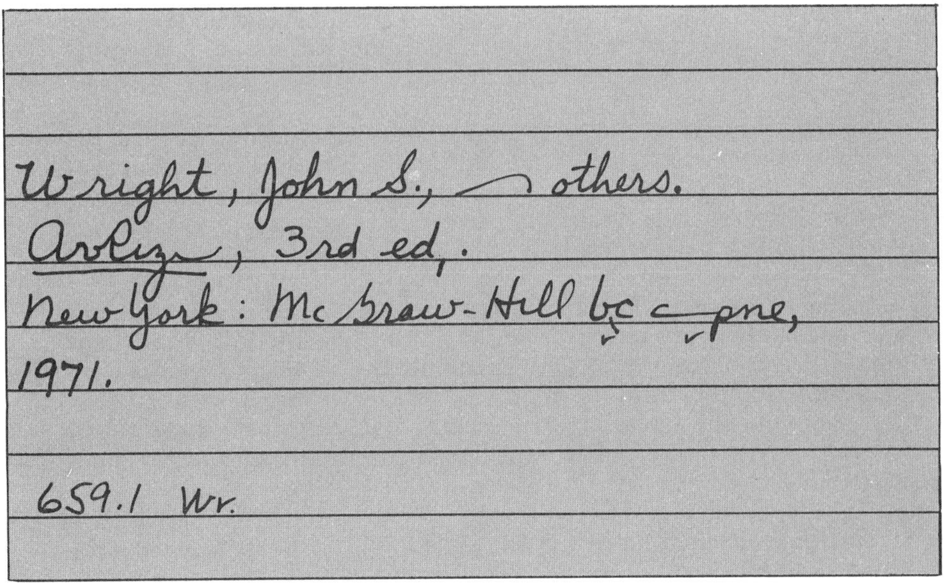

SAMPLE BIBLIOGRAPHY CARD

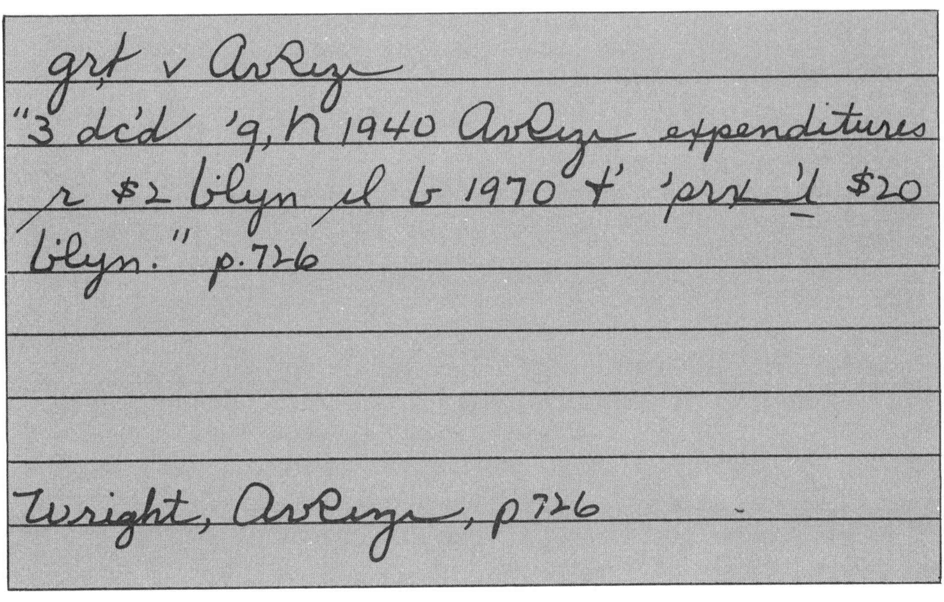

SAMPLE NOTE CARD

ESSENTIALS FOR NOTE CARDS

The information you write on each card will depend on the source of the note and on the way you think you will use it. Every note card should have the following items:

Source. Write the author's name and an abbreviated title at the bottom of each note card. Then, before you write a single note, get out your bibliography card and check the accuracy of the information on the card with the actual item. When you use note cards for your own ideas or as reminders, write "me" as the source.

Label or heading. Put a label on the top line of each note card. The label tells you where the note fits in your outline. Sometimes you will run across important information for which you have no provisions in your outline. In such cases, leave the label line blank and complete the rest of the note card. You may find that you will want to revise your outline to accommodate these unanticipated items.

The note itself. If your note consists of a verbatim quote (the author's exact words), put quotation marks around the note. If you restate or summarize a passage in your own words (paraphrase), omit the quotation marks. If your note is too long for the front side of the card, you may complete it on the reverse side, but the source should always be on the face of each note card. Because you limit each card to one item, you will often have several note cards for a single source. Keep these cards together until you are ready to sort them according to your outline.

Page numbers. The page number or numbers where the item is found is written after the source.

On the back of the card you may want to make notes to yourself about the particular source or about how you think the item can be used in your paper.

TO CONSIDER AND DISCUSS

1. Explain why you should take more notes than you can use.
2. Give 3 reasons why you should record each reading note on a separate card.
3. Give the 4 essential items that must be on each note card.

WRITING SHORTCUTS

Combination *ou-ow*. Write a small longhand *o* to express the combinations *ow-ou.* If you can learn to write the *o* in a clockwise direction, you will write faster.

As you read each of the words below, write the outline 3 times or until you can write it without hesitation. Practice reading and writing each word until all are mastered.

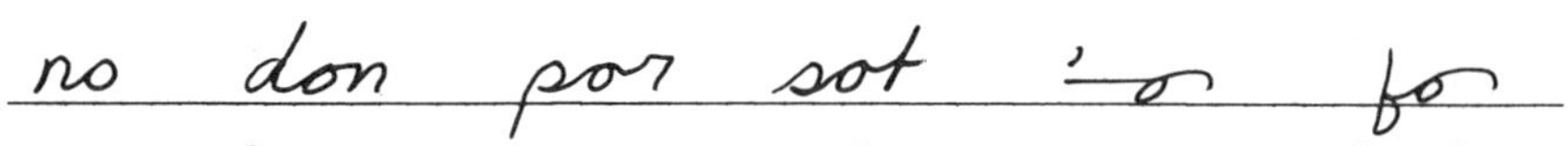

now **down** **power** **south** **amount** **found**

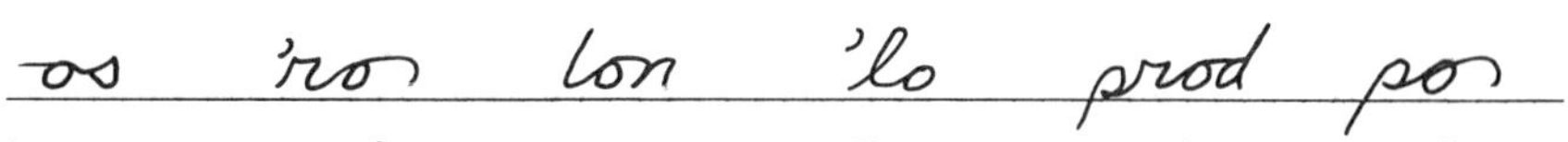

house **around** **town** **allow** **proud** **pound**

Prefix and suffix *out*. Write a small longhand *o* to express the prefix and the suffix *out*.

Cover the print and read the notes illustrating the prefix and suffix *out* until you can read the outlines as fast as you can read the print. Then cover the outlines and write each word as you read it from print. Try to read your own notes. If there are any words you cannot read, rewrite the outlines.

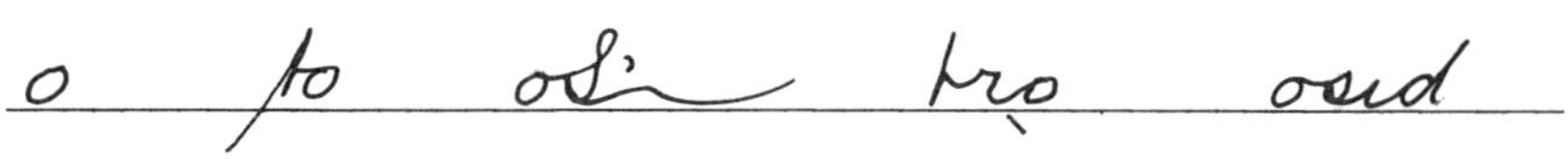

out **without** **outstanding** **throughout** **outside**

outline **outfit** **outlet** **outlined** **output**

Abbreviated words and phrases. Most fields of work and study have their own terms, phrases, abbreviations, and jargon. These special vocabularies are a form of "shorthand" that permit accurate and speedy communication. For example, the short-order cook knows precisely what to do when a waiter calls out, "A pair over easy!"

As you become familiar with terms used in a course, watch for expressions that are repeated with high frequency. If such terms or phrases are difficult to write, you should devise your own abbreviations. Shown below, for example, are some abbreviations that a student in European History has developed. Of course, you should not memorize these examples. They are given here to illustrate the idea.

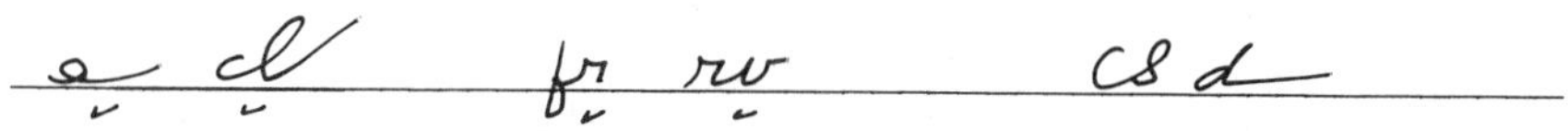

English colonies **French Revolution** **constitutional democracy**

NOTES TO READ AND WRITE

Read the following notes until you can read them without hesitation. Then turn to the key and write your own notes from the print. Say each sentence to yourself as you write it. Check your notes with those in the text.

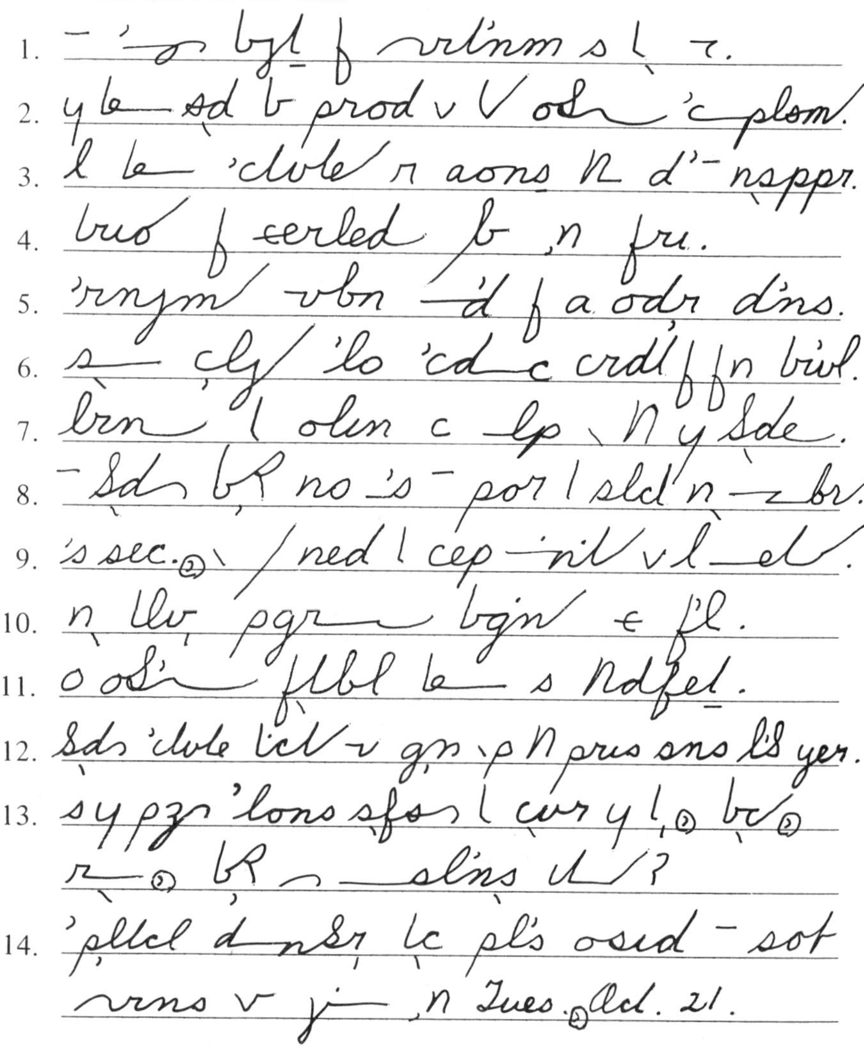

SPELLING PRACTICE

Check the spelling of each of the following words. They are among those most frequently misspelled by college freshmen. After you have studied the spelling of these words, write the outline for each word on a separate piece of paper. Then close your text and write out each word from the outline you have written. Check your spelling with the list in the text and review the words you misspelled.

develop	lose	whose
disappoint	maintenance	writing

PUNCTUATION REVIEW–THE DASH

The dash is useful to show a sharp break in a sentence and to introduce a surprise element. However, its overuse is common among beginning writers. They often use dashes when unsure of punctuation rules. Therefore, if in doubt about punctuation, don't reveal this fact by using dashes.

Rules for dashes. Use dashes to (a) show a sudden change or break in a sentence, (b) to set off a parenthetic group of words containing commas, or (c) before a summarizing statement.

The dash is written with no space between the dash and the preceding or following word. On a typewriter, you make a dash by striking 2 hyphens with no space between.

Examples. The sentences below include samples calling for each of the above rules. The letter following the sentence tells which rule applies.

1. I worked so hard–how could I lose? (a)
2. All major sports–football, basketball, and baseball–were canceled. (b)
3. A notebook, a pencil, and an eraser–these are all you will need for the test. (c)
4. Her performance on the piano was superb–but I am getting ahead of the story. (a)
5. The trips for school groups–to museums, galleries, and performances–are subsidized by the organization. (b)

NOTETAKING APPLICATIONS

1. Complete the self-checks in Unit 16 in your *Handbook*.
2. Use Tape 4 Side B from the *Notetaking Tape Library* to build speed. If the tapes are not available, your instructor will read the words and sentences to you while you take notes.
3. If time permits, complete the Optional Applications.

KEY TO *NOTES TO READ AND WRITE*

1. The amount budgeted for entertainment is too high.
2. Your team should be proud of its outstanding accomplishments. (20)
3. All team activities are announced in the daily newspaper.
4. Tryouts for cheerleading will be on Friday. (40)
5. Arrangements have been made for an outdoor dance.
6. Some colleges allow academic credit for foreign travel. (60)
7. Learning to outline can help you in your studying.
8. The student board now has the power to select new members. (80)
9. As secretary, you will need to keep minutes of all meetings.
10. New television programming begins each fall. (100)
11. Our outstanding football team is undefeated.
12. Student activity tickets have gone up in price since last year. (120)
13. Is your present allowance sufficient to cover your tuition, books, room, board and miscellaneous items. (140)
14. A political demonstration took place outside the south entrance of the gym on Tuesday, October 21. (160)

Chapter 17

PREPARING FOOTNOTES

The task of preparing footnotes strikes fear into the hearts of many beginning writers and researchers. However, if accurate and complete bibliography cards are prepared and care is taken to note page numbers on all note cards, the mysteries of footnoting are soon unraveled.

PURPOSES OF FOOTNOTES

Footnotes serve 2 main purposes. First, they help you "prove" your point. You use footnotes to demonstrate to your reader that you have consulted the writings of recognized authorities about the ideas or facts you present and that these authorities agree with you.

A second use of footnotes is to acknowledge that the idea or quotation is from another's work. If you do not give proper credit to a source you use, you are guilty of *plagiarism,* a form of literary theft. To support properly your points and to acknowledge the work of others, a footnote tells the exact source of a quotation, fact, or an idea so your reader can look up the original statement if he chooses to do so.

WHAT TO FOOTNOTE

You should footnote all important facts and statements of opinion that are not common knowledge. For example, you would footnote another's exact words (a quotation). You must also footnote another's ideas that you have summarized or restated in your own words. Even though the words are yours, you must acknowledge the source of the idea.

You do not footnote facts that are well-known and generally accepted. For example, you would not footnote the fact that there are seven continents or that the earth turns on its axis or that milers have run the mile in less than 4 minutes. If you are in doubt about whether or not to footnote an item, play safe and add the footnote.

PROPER FORM FOR FOOTNOTES

A footnote must include all the information needed to locate the item to which it refers. Therefore, the precise content and form of a footnote will depend on the nature of the source to which it refers.

Example of a footnote to a book. Here is an example of how to footnote a direct quotation from a book:

> In tracing the rapid growth of advertising in recent years, Wright concludes, "Three decades ago in 1940, advertising expenditures were $2 billion, while by 1970 they approximated $20 billion."[1]

The quotation marks shows that these are the exact words from the source. The small raised number after the closing quotation mark tells the reader that a footnote will give details about the source. Notice that the quotation was introduced by a statement indicating the significance of the quotation for this particular paper. Obviously, the author wants to convince the reader that the advertising business is a "growth" industry, and the quotation from an authority supports that idea.

At the foot of the page, the reader would find this footnote:

---

[1] John S. Wright and others, *Advertising* (New York: McGraw-Hill Book Company, 1971), p. 726.

With these facts about the book in the footnote, the curious reader could look up the quotation in Wright's book.

Note that the title of the book in the footnote above is set in italic type. In printed books, magazines, and other sources, all titles are set in italics. But when titles are typed, they are underlined because the standard typewriter does not have italic type.

Example of a second reference to a book. Once you have given a footnote for a work, you need not repeat the entire footnote when you refer to the same source a second time. Here is an example of how to footnote a later reference to Wright's book:

> Although the advertising business has grown rapidly in the past, there are no signs at present that this growth will level off. One authority predicts that advertising will continue to be a vital tool of business in the decades ahead.[3]

Because there are no quotation marks, your reader knows that the author has summarized or restated the words of others. If this passage is a summary or a restatement of another's words. A proper footnote for this second reference to a source would be as follows:

---

[3] Wright, p. 727.

This footnote tells your reader that this passage is from the Wright book. The absence of further identifying information indicates that complete footnote details are given earlier in the paper.

For examples of footnote and bibliography entries for 20 different types of material, see "A Writer's Guide to Bibliography and Footnotes" in your *Handbook.*

TO CONSIDER AND DISCUSS

1. Give 2 main purposes of footnotes.
2. Define *plagiarism* and explain how footnotes can help you avoid it.

NOTES TO READ AND WRITE

Read the following notes until you can read them without hesitation. Then turn to the key and write your own notes from the print. Say each sentence to yourself as you write it. Check your notes with those in the text.

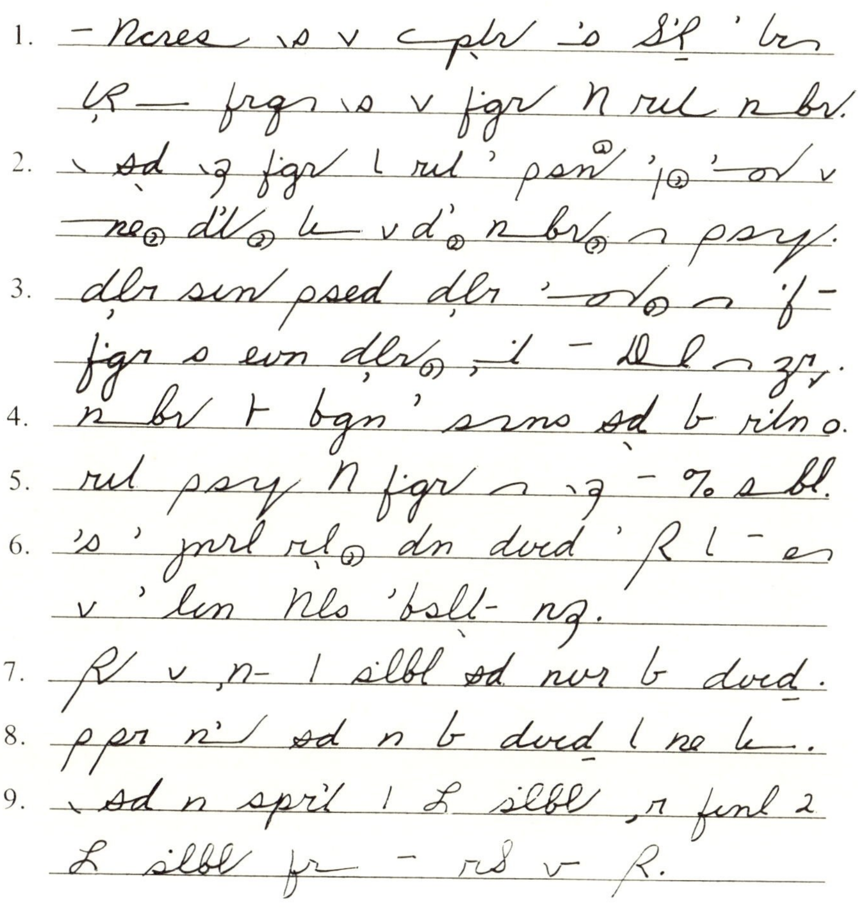

10. 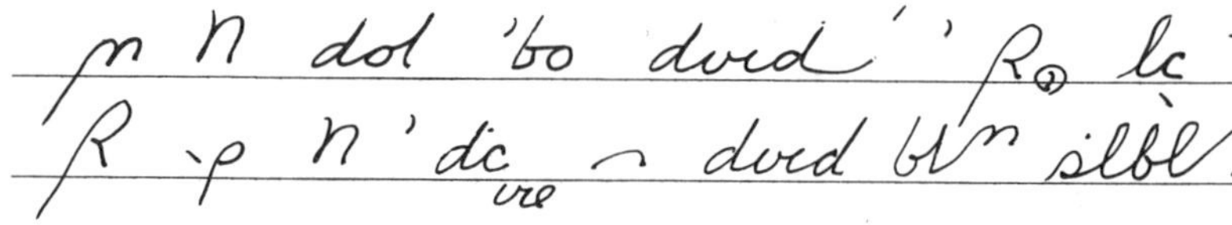

PUNCTUATION REVIEW–THE HYPHEN

The hyphen has many uses. It is used to divide words at the end of a line of type, to form compound words, to write out fractions, to join certain prefixes to a word, and in several other ways. We deal here only with the 2 most common rules for using the hyphen.

Rules for hyphens. Use a hyphen to (a) join 2 or more words used as a single descriptive word *before a noun,* and (b) to form certain compound nouns made up of 2 or more words.

Examples. The sentences below include illustrations of each of the above rules. The letter following the sentence tells which rule applies.

1. Mark Twain is a well-known author. (a)
2. Debbie worked at a drive-in on weekends. (b)
3. We were voting for secretary-treasurer. (b)
4. Please give step-by-step directions. (a)
5. We climbed to the top of the 10-story building. (a)
6. Will he be editor-in-chief next year? (b)
7. It is important to exercise self-control in a debate. (b)
8. Confirmation of the appointment required a two-thirds majority. (a)

Special caution. Do not hyphenate 2 or more descriptive words if they *follow* the noun. In the examples that follow, note how the hyphen is inserted only when the descriptive words precede the noun.

1. The political rally lasted 40 minutes.
2. It was a 40-minute political rally.
3. He reported information that is up to date.
4. He reported up-to-date information.

NOTETAKING APPLICATIONS

1. Complete the self-checks in Unit 17 in your *Handbook.*
2. Use Tape 4 Side B from the *Notetaking Tape Library* to build speed. If the tapes are not available, your instructor will read the words and sentences to you while you take notes.
3. If time permits, complete the Optional Applications.

KEY TO *NOTES TO READ AND WRITE*

1. The increasing use of computers has started a trend toward more frequent use of figures in writing numbers. (20)
2. You should use figures to write a person's age, amounts of money, dates, time of day, numbers, and percentages. (40)
3. Dollar signs precede dollar amounts, and if the figure is even dollars, omit the decimal and zeros. (60)
4. Numbers that begin a sentence should be written out.
5. Write percentages in figures and use the percent symbol. (80)
6. As a general rule, do not divide a word at the end of a line unless absolutely necessary. (100)
7. Words of only one syllable should never be divided.
8. Proper names should not be divided at any time. (120)
9. You should not separate one-letter syllables or final 2-letter syllables from the rest of the word. (140)
10. When in doubt about dividing a word, look the word up in a dictionary and divide between syllables. (160)

EXAMINATION 2

All the examinations are in the back of your *Handbook.* Each is to be removed along the perforation. When directed to do so by your instructor, remove and take Examination 2. This test covers the material that has been covered up to this point in your text and *Handbook.*

Chapter 18

WRITING YOUR PAPER

When working on a term paper, the time finally comes when you must stop reading and begin writing. Many students underestimate the time needed to finish a paper once the research and reading are done. Therefore, you should allow plenty of time to complete the steps discussed below.

REEXAMINE YOUR PURPOSES

As you have increased your knowledge of your topic and accumulated information, you may have changed your views considerably. Now is the time to set down in a sentence or 2 your purposes in writing the paper. For example, the purpose in writing a paper on "Career Opportunities in Advertising" might be stated: "The purpose of this paper is to examine and discuss the career opportunities in the advertising business."

PREPARE A WORKING OUTLINE

As a result of your reading, your preliminary outline has doubtless changed. Perhaps you have dropped some topics, added new headings, and rearranged others. By this time, you should have good-sized stack of note cards from your reading, interviews, and other research.

Group your note cards. Group those cards together that have the same label. If your note cards do not seem to fall into a logical organization, examine them closely to see if the labels should be revised. Considerable shuffling and rearranging may be required. You may find that you have insufficient data to support some points you want to make. If so, you may have to do some additional research and reading.

Number your note cards. With your note cards grouped into major categories, put a large Roman numeral I on all cards under the heading that will come first in your paper; put a Roman II on the second group, and so on. Then arrange the cards under Roman I in the order you will present the material they cover and rearrange the cards under the other headings.

Make a sentence outline. When your cards are in proper order, your working outline almost writes itself. Your outline will be much easier to use in writing your paper if you make a sentence rather than a topic outline.

START WRITING

Where is a good place to begin your writing? Don't start with your introduction. Write it last when you will have a better idea of what you are introducing.

Begin with a major heading. Look at your working outline and pick the major heading that you feel will be easiest to write. Then plunge right in. Don't be concerned at this point about your writing style. The main thing is to get started.

Use your notetaking skill. Jot down your main points as quickly as possible so you can think about them. Write on only one side of each sheet and leave at least one blank line between each line of writing so that you can add ideas as they occur to you. Number each sheet.

Attach your note cards. As you write, indicate where you will use the material from your note cards and clip each card to the sheet where it will be used. If you follow this plan, you will use each note card only once.

Weave quotations into your own writing. Your paper must include your own ideas and judgments as well as those of the authorities you quote. You cannot simply string a series of quotations together and have an acceptable paper. You must combine your own words with quotations and material from your sources to give your reader a fluent blend of ideas.

REWRITE AND POLISH

Professional writers agree that a secret of good writing is rewriting. So do not expect your first draft to be a finished product. Many experienced writers rewrite many times before they are satisfied.

After you have finished your draft, put it aside overnight. A waiting period before the final rewrite will give you a better perspective on ways to improve your paper. Then read your draft carefully, revise and rewrite. As you rewrite, use scissors and paste to shift material that does not require rewriting.

Write the introduction. After you feel the body of your paper is as good as you can make it, begin work on your introduction. Remember, opening paragraphs are sure to be read and they give that important first impression to your instructor or other reader. Therefore, you should devote extra time and thought to your introduction. Use it to get your reader's attention by doing one or more of the following:

1. Indicate the importance of the topic.
2. Tell why your topic is timely.

3. Tell your reader how you will deal with your topic.
4. Give an anecdote to illustrate your approach or to lead directly into your topic.

Write the conclusion. As with the introduction, time spent on the final paragraphs can make a significant difference in a reader's assessment of a term paper. Even if your instructor does not have time to read every word of every term paper, you may be sure that your conclusion will be read. Here is where you tell what you learned from your research. In your conclusion, you will probably want to restate your purpose in doing the research and tell how your findings have contributed to that purpose.

Type the final draft. Before typing the paper in final form, read it through 3 times and concentrate on a different aspect with each reading. First, read it to make sure that you have a smooth flow of ideas from paragraph to paragraph. Read it a second time to check your sentence structure and punctuation. The third time through, check the spelling of each word. Then type your paper on a good bond (not thin) paper. A complete guide to typing a term paper is given in your *Handbook* in "A Writer's Guide to Format."

TO CONSIDER AND DISCUSS

1. Explain why introductions and conclusions are so important in writing term and research papers.
2. Explain why an outline is likely to change as you work on a term paper.
3. Be prepared to discuss one specific problem you have encountered when writing a term paper and tell how you feel the suggestions in this chapter might help you with that problem in the future.

WRITING SHORTCUTS

Sound of *oi-oy*. Write a dotted *i* to express the sound *oi-oy*.

Read the following words. When you can read the first line fluently, cover the notes and write each note as you read from the print. Do this until you can write each word rapidly and accurately. Check your notes. Follow the same procedure for the second line.

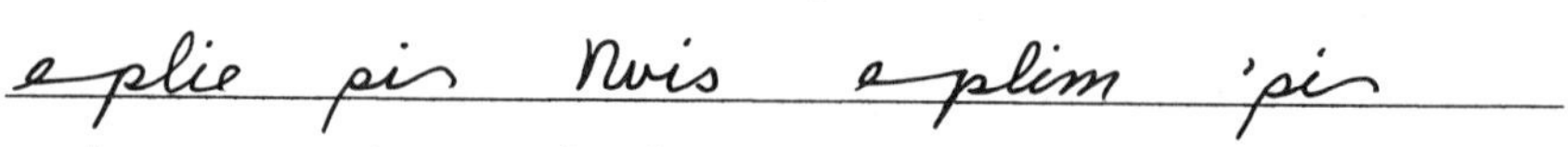

employee **point** **invoice** **employment** **appoint**

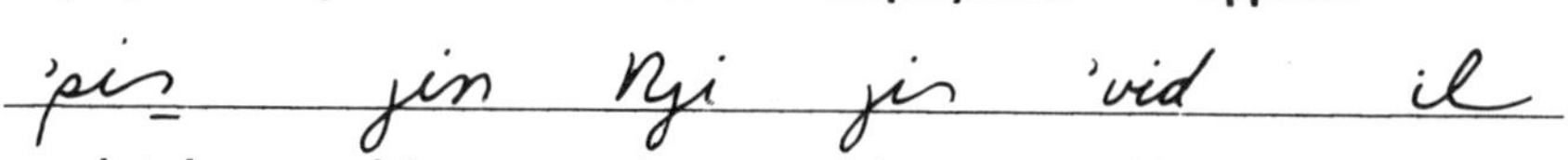

appointed **join** **enjoy** **joint** **avoid** **oiling**

NOTES TO READ AND WRITE

Read the following notes until you can read them without hesitation. Then turn to the key and write your own notes from the print. Say each sentence to yourself as you write it. Check your notes with those in the text.

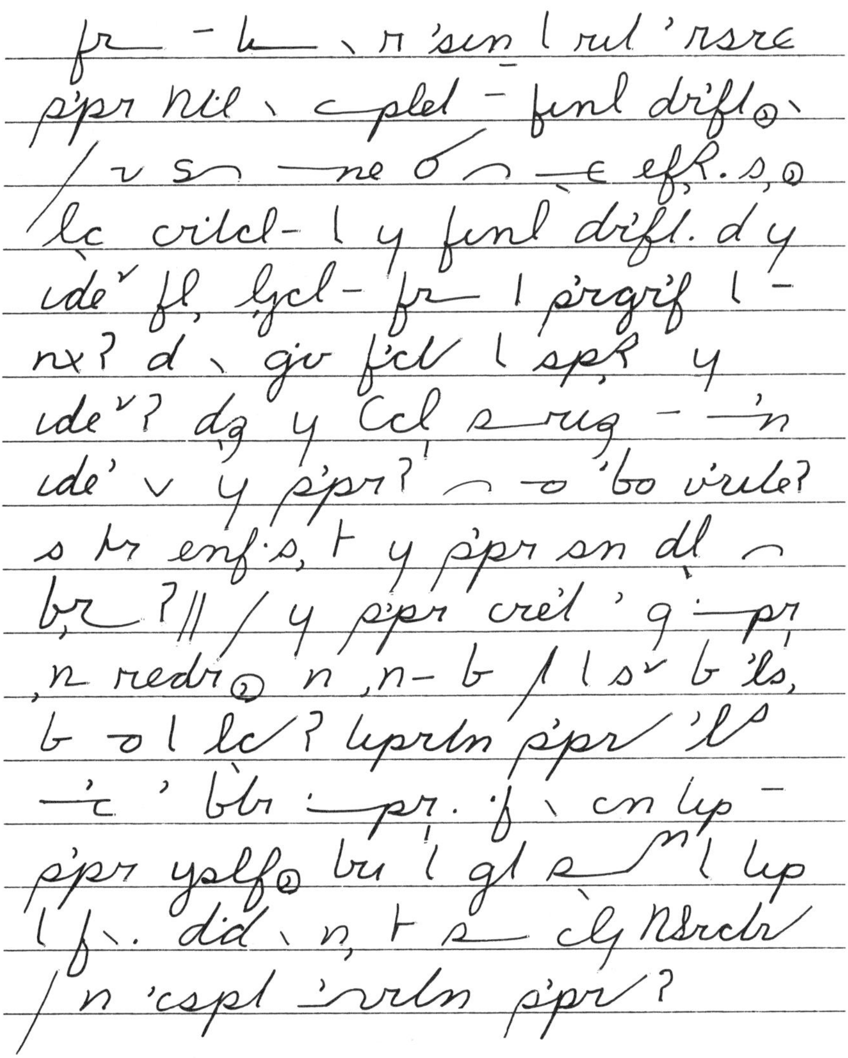

PUNCTUATION REVIEW–ELLIPSES

When quoting from the works of others, you will often want to omit words, phrases, or entire sentences. To do so, you must use ellipses (rhymes with *lips ease).*

Rules for ellipses. Use an ellipsis mark to indicate that part of a quotation has been omitted. If the omission occurs at the beginning or in the middle of a sentence, use 3 periods in the ellipsis. If the last part of a sentence is omitted or if entire sentences are omitted, add a fourth period to the ellipsis to mark the end of the sentence.

Examples. Note how omitted material is indicated by ellipses in the quotations that follow:

1. "Give me liberty . . . or death." (The ellipsis shows that "or give me" has been omitted.)
2. The *Magna Charta* states: "No freeman shall be . . . imprisoned . . . save by the lawful judgment of his peers. . . ." (The 3-dot ellipsis shows that words in the middle of the sentence have been omitted. The 4-dot ellipsis shows that words at the end of the sentence have been left out.)

SPELLING PRACTICE

Check the spelling of each of the following words. They are among those most frequently misspelled by college freshmen. After you have studied the spelling of these words, write the outline for each word on a separate piece of paper. Then close your text and write out each word from the outline you have written. Check your spelling with the list in the text and review the words you misspelled.

accidentally	irrelevant	procedure
advise	laboratory	proceed
already	led	professor

NOTETAKING APPLICATIONS

1. Complete the self-checks in Unit 18 in your *Handbook.*
2. Use Tape 5 Side A from the *Notetaking Tape Library* to build speed. If the tapes are not available, your instructor will read the words and sentences to you while you take notes.
3. If time permits, complete the Optional Applications.

KEY TO *NOTES TO READ AND WRITE*

From the time you are assigned to write a research paper until you complete the final draft, you will have spent (20) many hours and much effort. So look critically at your final draft. Do your ideas flow logically from (40) one paragraph to the next? Do you give facts to support your ideas? Does your conclusion summarize the main (60) idea of your paper? And how about variety? Is there enough so that your paper is not dull and boring? (80)

Will your paper create a good impression on the reader, not only by what it says but also by how (100) it looks? Typewritten papers always make a better impression. If you cannot type the paper yourself, try to (120) get someone to type it for you. Did you know that some college instructors will not accept handwritten papers? (139)

Chapter 19

PROOFREADING

By the time you have finished typing a paper, you may hope never to look at it again. But you should. One of the most important steps of all is your final checking and proofreading.

A careless typographical error or a misnumbered footnote can seriously affect a reader's judgment of a paper that is superb in every other way. Try, therefore, to muster the discipline and determination required to proofread carefully.

Distinction between checking and proofreading. These words—checking and proofreading—may have the same meaning to you. But there are differences. To *check* is to insure over-all accuracy; to *proofread* is to read specifically for making corrections. Thus, proofreading is a specialized aspect of checking. Usually, it is the last step in preparing a paper.

If you think proofreading is a demanding job, you are right. It requires a high level of concentration. Here are some hints that may help you to proofread more effectively.

Allow time to proofread. You can hardly be attentive to the task of proofreading if you leave the final reading of your paper until the moment before you turn it in. Furthermore, even if you find an error, you may not have a typewriter with which to correct it. Try to schedule your time so that you can proofread in an unhurried way.

Proofread in a quiet place. A bustling study hall or a school bus are obviously not ideal places to proofread. Try to find a place where you can work without disturbance or interruption.

Compare with original sources. Read the material over carefully, comparing it to the original so you can check numbers and the like with their original source. Be particularly alert for passages that don't seem to make sense.

Read in pairs. One person reads aloud from the original, the other person—the copyholder—follows along checking the new copy. The reader should read punctuation marks, indicate paragraphing, and spell out troublesome words and proper names.

Use a tape recorder. If you must proofread alone, use modern technology to help. Read the original to the tape recorder, then play back the recording while you check the copy.

Checking numbers. If you are proofreading tables that include columns of numbers, it is easier to check them by reading down the columns.

PROOFREADERS' MARKS

Proofreaders' marks are shorthand instructions for making corrections in typewritten or printed matter. The marks are understood by all typesetters and many typists. You should learn to use the marks to make corrections because they save writing out instructions that would require time and space.

Here are the most common proofreaders' marks. The typewritten passage on the following page has been corrected with these marks to show how they are used.

- Delete
- Insert additions or something omitted
- Insert quotation marks
- Insert a comma
- Insert space
- Lower case
- Close up
- Capitalize
- Move right
- Move left
- Move up
- Move down
- Transpose words or letters
- Paragraph
- Insert period
- Underline or italics
- Let it stand

TO CONSIDER AND DISCUSS

1. Explain the distinction between proofreading and checking.
2. How do careless errors affect a reader's assessment of a paper.
3. Bring an example of a typographical error from a magazine or newspaper and be prepared to show how you would correct it. Use the proper proofreaders' mark.

WE REMEMBER wHEN]

cap. ¶ When the first United States airline was started, the
ℊ public could be forgiven for ~~for~~ approaching air
travel with less than zeal. The airplane of 1926
^ was designed to carry mail, not people and many pas-
⁀ sengers found themselves rid ing on top of mail sacks,
in undoubtedly feeling very brave the goggles, helmets,
windjackets, and hot water bottles thoughtfully provided by the airline. A passenger had a right to
ital. [feel brave, for that matter; he was. The career
\# expectancy ofa pilot in those days was an optimistic
five years. Of the first 40 pilots hired by the U.S.
tr. Post Office Department in 1919, 31 were daed by 1925,
⊙ all in crashes

tr. With mail furnishing the bulk of airline icnome,
⁀ it was no wonder that some oper ators resorted to
ingenious methods of increasing such revenue. The
Cap/# Post office paid by poundage carried. Onecarrier
l.c. noted happily that wet Blotters weighed twice as much
⊙ as dry blotters Another airline thought up the idea
of wrapping bricks in ordinary paper and sending them
tr. mail air--at $3 per pound. This lucrative gimmick
l.c. collapsed when a new employee, not briefed on Proper
ℊ brick-mailing techniques, merely tied an ~~an~~ address
^ label on a nude brick attached an air mail stamp to
the label, and sent it to another city--where a postal
inspector intercepted it.[1]

---

tr. Robert J. Serling, "We Remember When, Mainliner, April, 1971, p. 7. Reporduced with permission of United Air Lines.

WRITING SHORTCUTS

Prefixes *ax-ex-ox*. Write a long, straight, slanted, downward stroke to express *ax, ex,* and *ox*. Be sure to slant the stroke so it looks like half of an *x*.

Cover the print of each line of words and read the notes until you can read them as fast as you can the print. Write each word and try to read your notes. Then increase your writing rate on the words by scribble writing each word several times. Remember to say each word as you write it.

express **export** **extend-extent** **experience** **exist**

expect **examination** **excellent** **explain** **expense**

except **oxide** **axle** **examine**

Combination *extr*. Write a small longhand x to express the *extr.*

As you read each outline, write it 3 times. Do this for all the words.

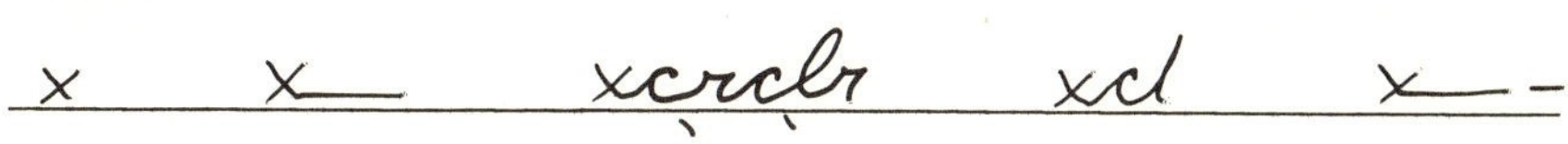

extra **extreme** **extracurricular** **extract** **extremely**

NOTES TO READ AND WRITE

Read the following notes until you can read them without hesitation. Then turn to the key and write your own notes from the print. Say each sentence to yourself as you write it. Check your notes with those in the text.

1.
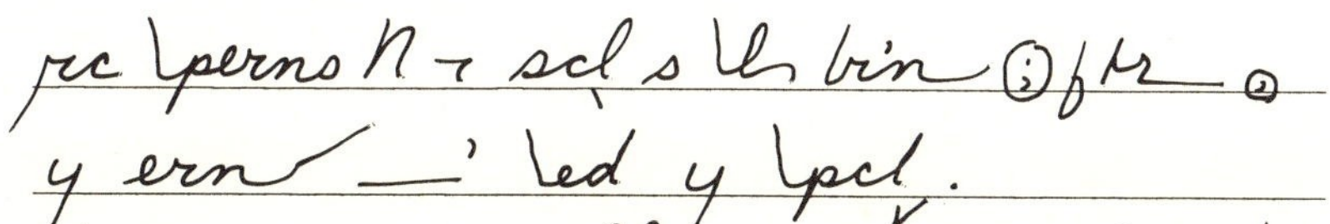

2.
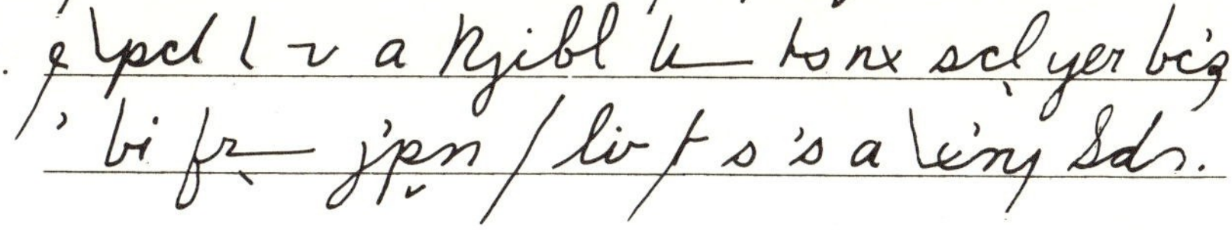

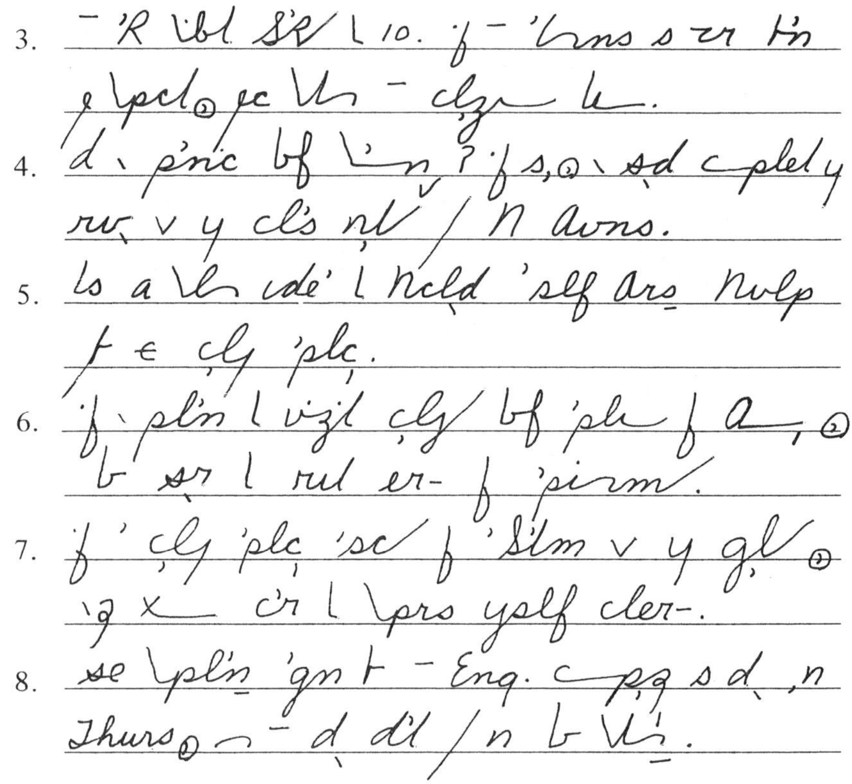

SPELLING PRACTICE

Check the spelling of each of the following words. They are among those most frequently misspelled by college freshmen. After you have studied the spelling of these words, write the outline for each word on a separate piece of paper. Then close your text and write out each word from the outline you have written. Check your spelling with the list in the text and review the words you misspelled.

analysis	loneliness	pursue
arguing	marriage	pursuit
beginning	meant	quantity

PUNCTUATION REVIEW—THE COLON

You will recall that the colon has several uses. It separates hours from minutes in writing times (8:50 a.m.). You use it in footnotes (New Haven: Yale University Press, 1977). A colon also follows the salutation in formal correspondence (Dear Dean Rogers:).

Other rules for the use of the colon. In your own notetaking and writing, you will probably use the colon most frequently (a) to introduce a series of items or (b) to introduce a formal statement, quotation, or question. The letter after each example indicates the rule that applies.

1. Three teams participated in the track meet: Mankato, Bemidji, and Moorhead. (a)
2. She named her four favorite classical composers: Beethoven, Brahms, Mozart, and Bach. (a)
3. This we believe: Inflation will not subside until government spending declines and industrial productivity increases. (b) (Note that a complete sentence following a colon begins with a capital.)
4. This is the question before the council: Should money be appropriated for a new school library or for a new gym? (b)
5. Be sure to pack the following items for the camping trip: sleeping bag, fishing gear, mess kit, first aid kit, and flashlight. (a)
6. Step-by-step instructions for starting the car are as follows: (1) insert the key in the ignition, (2) check to see that the car is in neutral or "park," (3) set the parking brake, (4) fasten the seat belt, and (5) turn the ignition key. (a) (Note that letters or numbers may be used to designate the items in a series.)

NOTETAKING APPLICATIONS

1. Complete the self-checks in Unit 19 in your *Handbook.*
2. Use **Tape 5 Side A** from the *Notetaking Tape Library* to build speed. If the tapes are not available, your instructor will read the words and sentences to you while you take notes.
3. If time permits, complete the Optional Applications.

KEY TO *NOTES TO READ AND WRITE*

1. Work experience in high school is excellent training; furthermore, your earnings may exceed your expectations. (20)
2. We expect to have an enjoyable time this next school year because a boy from Japan will live with us as an exchange student. (40)
3. The art exhibit starts at 10. If the attendance is higher than we expect, we can extend the closing time. (60)
4. Do you panic before examinations? If so, you should complete your review of your class notes well in advance. (80)
5. It is an excellent idea to include a self-addressed envelope with each college application. (100)
6. If you plan to visit colleges before applying for admission, be sure to write early for appointments. (120)
7. If a college application asks for a statement of your goals, use extreme care to express yourself clearly. (140)
8. She explained again that the English composition is due on Thursday, and the due date will not be extended. (160)

Chapter 20

MAKING COLLEGE APPLICATIONS

Most of today's high school graduates go on to some sort of postsecondary education at some time in their lives. Many go right on without interruption; others postpone further education for a period of work or service.

Whether you decide to go right on to college or to delay college entrance, the chances are good that you will go on at some time in the future. Once you have decided to continue your education, you will be faced with decisions such as the following:

What type of institution? A community college? A vocational or technical school that provides training for a specific job? A 4-year program in the liberal arts? A preprofessional college program?

Which specific institution?

What field for a major?

Parents, guidance counselors, teachers, fellow students, and others can help you to make these decisions, but in the end, where you finally go and your field of study is up to you and to the institution of your choice.

CHECKLIST OF STEPS

Obviously, many factors will shape your decision, and they cannot all be presented in depth and detail here. Nevertheless, the steps listed below can help you to gather the information you need to make important decisions about your advanced education:

1. Discuss your tentative career goals with your guidance counselor to get suggestions as to the type of educational institution that will best meet your needs.
2. Look at college catalogs in your school or public library or write to several colleges to obtain recent catalogs and other information.
3. Meet with college representatives if they visit your school. If your school sponsors a "career day," plan to participate.
4. As you narrow down your choices, study entrance requirements carefully. Can you meet them? What examinations are required? When and where are they given?

5. Try to arrange to visit your top choices. When planning a visitation, write to the admissions office to arrange for interviews. If personal visits are not possible, talk with a person in your community who is familiar with the college. Recent graduates can often give you helpful information.
6. Prepare a detailed financial plan. The plan should show estimates of both your financial support as well as a budget of expenses. Show support, if any, that your parents will provide, savings that can be tapped, estimated income from summer jobs and part-time work, scholarship support, and the like. Your expense budget should include the following items: tuition, fees, books, room and board, travel, incidentals. College catalogs often include sample budgets against which you can check your estimates.
7. Is the institution in a location you like?
8. Does the available housing seem suitable? If you visit a college, be sure to ask to see the dormitories.
9. What financial assistance is available? How do you qualify? Visit the office of financial assistance when you visit the college of your choice.
10. If income from part-time work is included in your financial plan, survey these possibilities when you visit a college. Most colleges offer students assistance in getting work.
11. What is the deadline date for receipt of your application for admission? Multiple applications are often worth the work and expense if you have several choices or if you are unsure that you will be accepted by the college of your choice.

IMPORTANCE OF EARLY APPLICATION

Many colleges are hard pressed to process quickly the applications that flood their admissions offices on or near the deadline date. Similarly, guidance counselors and other advisors have less time for thoughtful attention to your needs as deadlines approach. It is extremely important, therefore, to begin your application process early.

TO CONSIDER AND DISCUSS

1. Using your notetaking skill, draft a letter to a college asking for admissions forms, a catalog, and information about financial aid.
2. Draft a letter to a college indicating that you are planning a visit and indicate the offices you would like to visit.
3. Give at least 2 reasons why it is desirable to begin the college application process early.

WRITING SHORTCUTS

Prefixes and suffixes *over* and *other*. Write a joined or disjoined capital *O* to express the prefixes *over* and *other.*

As you read each outline, write it 3 times. Do this for all words. When you can write all the words fluently, cover the outlines and write each word once from the print. Try to read your own notes.

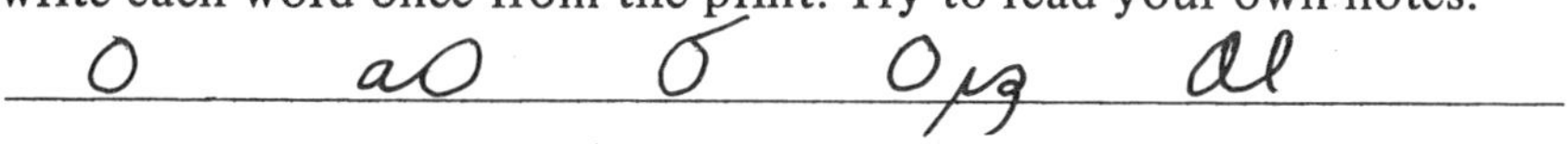

over-other **another** **others** **otherwise** **overall**

Prefix *trans.* Write a capital *T* to express the prefix *trans.*

Try to read the following notes as fast as you can read the print. Then write the outlines from the print and read them back. If any of your notes are difficult to read, rewrite them and read them again.

transfer **transferring** **transform** **transmit** **transact**

NOTES TO READ AND WRITE

Read the following notes until you can read them without hesitation. Then turn to the key and write your own notes from the print. Say each sentence to yourself as you write it. Check your notes with those in the text.

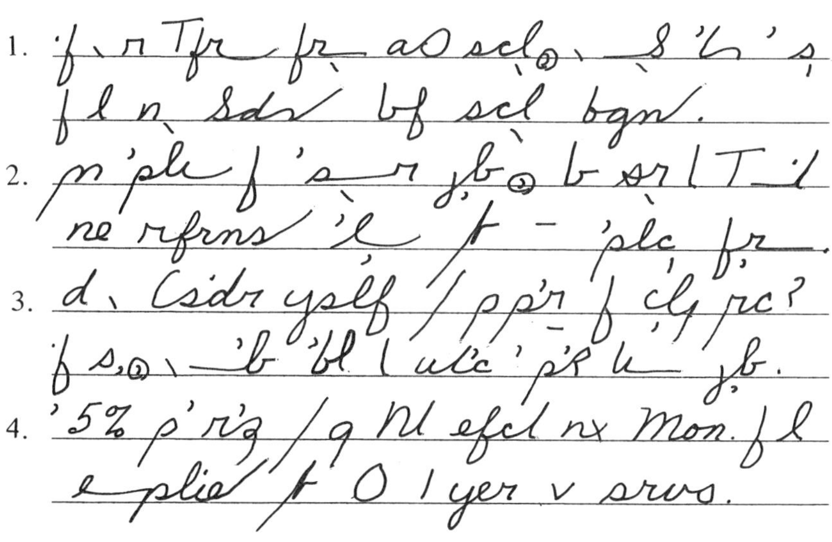

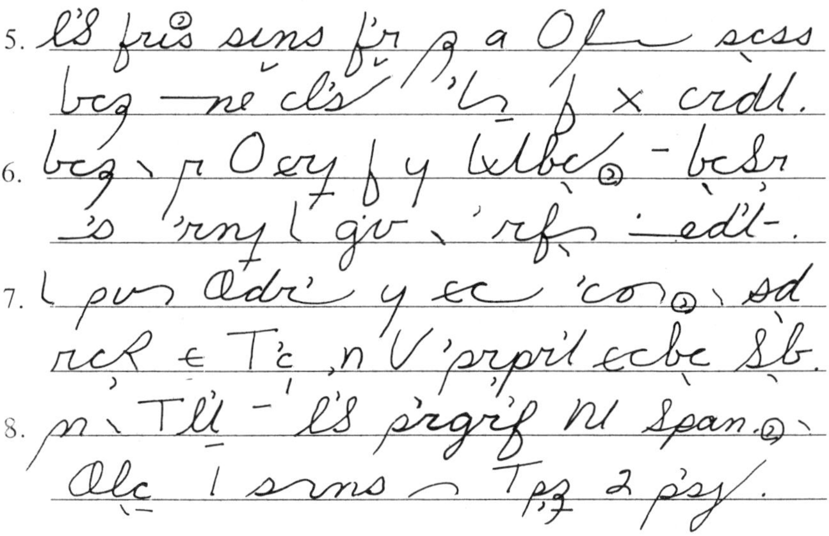

PUNCTUATION REVIEW–COMPOUND SENTENCES

You probably know that a *compound sentence* consists of 2 or more sentences that are combined into a single sentence. You may not recall, however, that there are 3 ways to form a compound sentence.

This review will show you how you can pack more ideas into your sentences by compounding. If you cannot form compound sentences, your writing will be like that of a child–a string of short, choppy sentences.

Rules for forming and punctuating compound sentences. Two or more whole sentences may be joined in 3 different ways to form a compound sentence.

a. Two whole sentences may be joined with a comma plus one of these connecting words: *and, but, for, or, either, neither,* and *nor.* This is the most common way to form compound sentences.

b. Two whole sentences may be joined with a semicolon plus a transitional word or phrase. Common transitional words and phrases include the following: *accordingly, however, therefore, consequently, in fact, hence, then, so, even so, still, finally, as a matter of fact,* etc. A transitional word must be followed by a comma.

c. Two or more whole sentences may be joined with a semicolon *without* a connecting word or a transitional word.

Examples. So you can compare the various ways of forming compound sentences, each of the examples below shows sentences joined in 3 ways.

1. John overestimated his gas mileage. He ran out of gas before he got to the beach. (two sentences)
2. John overestimated his gas mileage, and he ran out of gas before he got to the beach. (comma plus connecting word)
3. John overestimated his gas mileage; consequently, he ran out of gas before he got to the beach. (semicolon plus transitional word and comma)
4. John overestimated his gas mileage; he ran out of gas before he got to the beach. (semicolon alone)
5. The Blue Jays are a good baseball team. They have won most of their games this year. (two sentences)
6. The Blue Jays are a good baseball team, and they have won most of their games this year. (comma plus connecting word)
7. The Blue Jays are a good baseball team; in fact, they have won most of their games this year. (semicolon plus transitional word and comma)
8. The Blue Jays are a good baseball team; they have won most of their games this year. (semicolon alone)
9. The book was absorbing. I did not like the ending. (2 sentences)
10. The book was absorbing, but I did not like the ending. (semicolon plus connecting word)
11. The book was absorbing; even so, I did not like the ending. (semicolon plus transitional word and comma)

Special caution. Beginning writers are sometimes tempted to put a comma before *and* and *or* because they think they may have a compound sentence. Remember, you must have 2 whole sentences in order to have a compound sentence. To learn to identify compound sentences, study the sentences and the explanations that follow:

1. The campers went on hikes during the day, and they went on canoe trips at night. (This is a compound sentence because you could put a period after *day* and have 2 complete sentences).
2. The campers went on hikes during the day and on canoe trips at night. (This is not a compound sentence because "and on canoe trips at night" is not a complete sentence. There is no comma before *and* because *and* does not join 2 whole sentences.)

NOTETAKING APPLICATIONS

1. Complete the self-checks in Unit 20 in your *Handbook*.
2. Use Tape 5 Side B from the *Notetaking Tape Library* to build speed. If the tapes are not available, your instructor will read the words and sentences to you while you take notes.
3. If time permits, complete the Optional Applications.

KEY TO *NOTES TO READ AND WRITE*

1. If you are transferring from another school, you must attend a session for all new students before school begins. (20)
2. When applying for a summer job, be sure to transmit any references along with the application form. (40)
3. Do you consider yourself well prepared for college work? If so, you may be able to undertake a part-time job. (60)
4. A 5% pay raise will go into effect next Monday for all employees with over one year of service. (80)
5. Last Friday's Science Fair was an overwhelming success because many classes attended for extra credit. (100)
6. Because you were overcharged for your textbooks, the bookstore has arranged to give you a refund immediately. (120)
7. To prevent overdrawing your checking account, you should record each transaction on its appropriate checkbook stub. (140)
8. When you translated the last paragraph into Spanish, you overlooked one sentence and transposed 2 passages. (160)

Chapter 21

TAKING MINUTES OF MEETINGS

"Madam President, before we vote on the motion, please ask the Secretary to repeat the motion." If the Secretary is an effective notetaker, the motion will be read back exactly as it was offered.

THE SECRETARY'S DUTIES

If you are secretary of a club, committee, or similar organization, you will be expected to make the official record of the meetings. This record is called the *minutes* of the meeting. Your notetaking skill can help you take minutes.

Note details about the meeting. Minutes should include the time, date, and place of the meeting as well as the name of the presiding officer. Be sure to record this information for inclusion in the minutes of every meeting.

Identify the participants. If the group is small or if a minimum number is needed to conduct business, you should record the names of those present. As the official recorder of the proceedings, you will also be expected to record the names of people who make reports, motions, seconds, and the like. If you do not know their names, ask for identification.

An agenda helps. Many organizations distribute an agenda (a list of items to be discussed) a few days prior to a meeting. An agenda can serve as a guide to recording minutes, particularly in meetings where the agenda is closely followed.

Prepare for 2 types of materials. The minutes of most meetings include both verbatim material and summaries in the secretary's own words. The secretary summarizes the reports made by committees and the points discussed. But motions and other official actions are usually recorded verbatim to assure accuracy and to avoid future misunderstanding. For example, you should make a verbatim record of the corrections of minutes of a previous meeting, motions and resolutions passed, and other official statements of your organization.

Strive for accuracy. Because the minutes of a meeting must report accurately what has taken place, you should never hesitate to ask a speaker to repeat or clarify remarks.

Your minutes will be more accurate if you review all notes taken shortly after each meeting, making sure that you have all details needed to prepare the official minutes. Then type and distribute the minutes as soon as possible thereafter. Do not discard your notes after you have typed the minutes. You may want to refer to them when approval of the minutes is sought at the next meeting.

CONTENTS OF MINUTES

The minutes of a meeting usually contain the information that follows:

1. The name of the organization.
2. The kind of meeting (regular, annual, special, etc.).
3. The time, date, and place of the meeting.
4. Names of those present if the group is small or if a minimum number of members must be present to make the meeting official. Most organizations do not list members absent.
5. The name and title of the presiding officer.
6. A record of reports made, motions or resolutions presented, and their disposition. It is a common practice to note in the minutes the names of those who made reports, motions, and resolutions as well as those who seconded each item.
7. The minutes of some organizations include a summary of the discussion that precedes the vote on motions, but other organizations omit these details in their minutes.
8. The outcome of every vote should be recorded as either passed (or carried) or not passed (or failed). The actual tally is usually not recorded although unanimous votes are usually designated as such. ("The motion passed unanimously.")
9. The time the meeting was adjourned and the date and time of the next regular or special meeting.
10. The secretary signs the official copy of the minutes.

You will find a model format for typing minutes of meetings in "A Writer's Guide to Format" in your *Handbook*.

Special vocabulary for recording meetings. If you are called upon to record minutes of a meeting, you should review the following terms. Notetaking outlines, definitions, and examples of usage are given below.

An **agenda** is a list of things to be considered and is often sent to members of a group before a meeting. "We have a full agenda for tonight's meeting."

A **quorum** is the number of members of a body that must be present in order legally to conduct business (usually a majority). "The meeting was cancelled because we did not have a quorum."

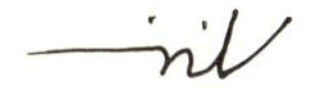

Minutes are the official record of the proceedings of a meeting. "The minutes were sent to each member."

Bylaws are a set of rules adopted by a group to govern its members and its affairs.

A **motion** is a formal proposal. One makes a motion by saying, "I move that . . ."

To **second** is to support a motion or a nomination. "I second the motion."

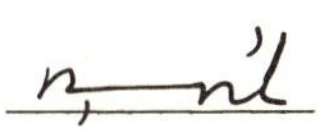

To **nominate** is to propose someone as a candidate for election to office.

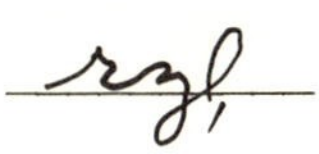

A **resolution** is an expression of opinion or intent voted by a body. "The resolution reads, 'Be it resolved that the Student Council supports the efforts of the Physical Education Department to secure better facilities for women's athletic activities.' "

TO CONSIDER AND DISCUSS

1. What items of business in a meeting usually require verbatim recording? Why?
2. Indicate the procedures a secretary should follow to help assure the accuracy of minutes.

WRITING SHORTCUTS

Prefix *ever-every* and suffix *ever*. Write a disjoined capital V for the word *ever* and the prefixes and suffixes *ever* and *every*.

Cover the print and read the notes until you can read the outlines as fast as you can read the print. Then cover the outlines and write each word as you read it from print. Try to read your own notes. If there are any words you cannot read, rewrite the outlines.

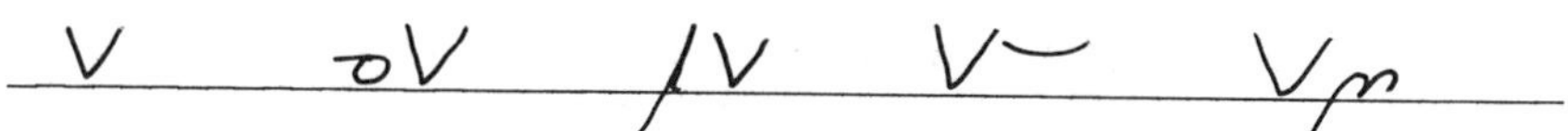

ever-every **however** **whatever** **everything** **everyone**

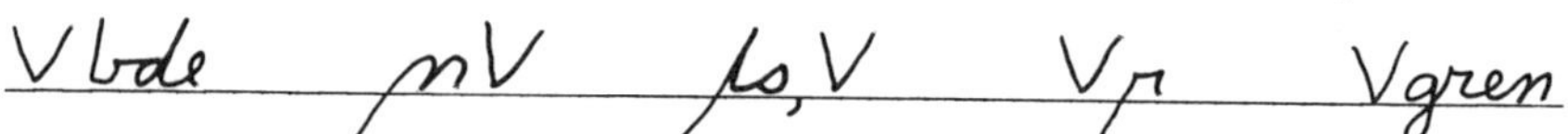

everybody **whenever** **whatsoever** **everywhere** **evergreen**

NOTES TO READ AND WRITE

Read the following notes until you can read them without hesitation. Then turn to the key and write your own notes from the print. Say each sentence to yourself as you write it. Check your notes with those in the text.

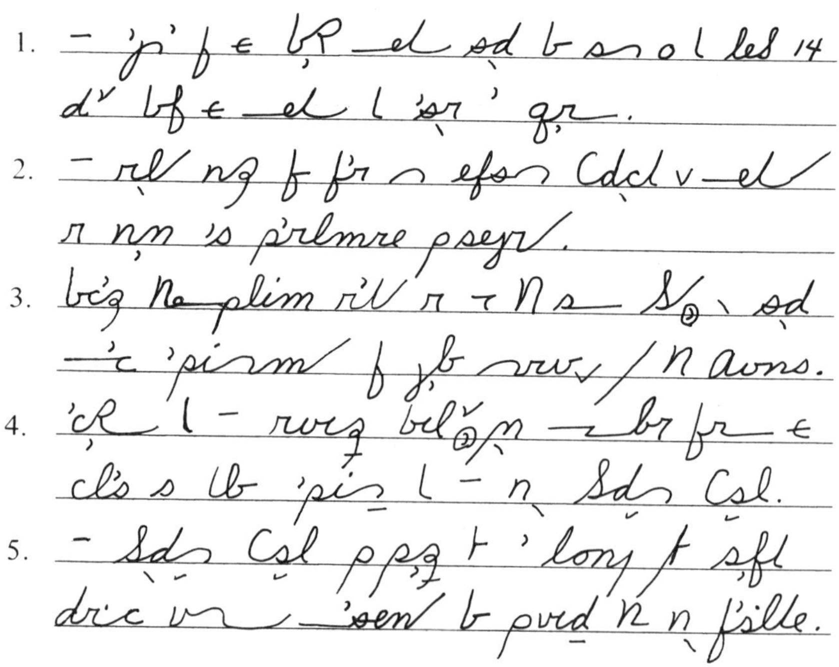

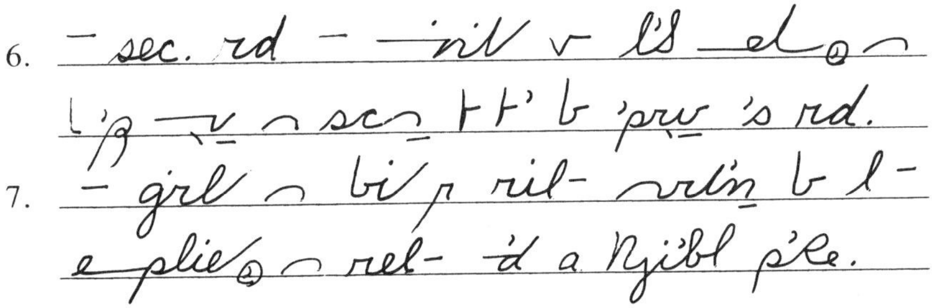

MORE NOTES TO READ AND WRITE

Read the following notes until you can read them without hesitation. Then turn to the key and write your own notes from the print. Say each sentence to yourself as you write it. Check your notes with those in the text.

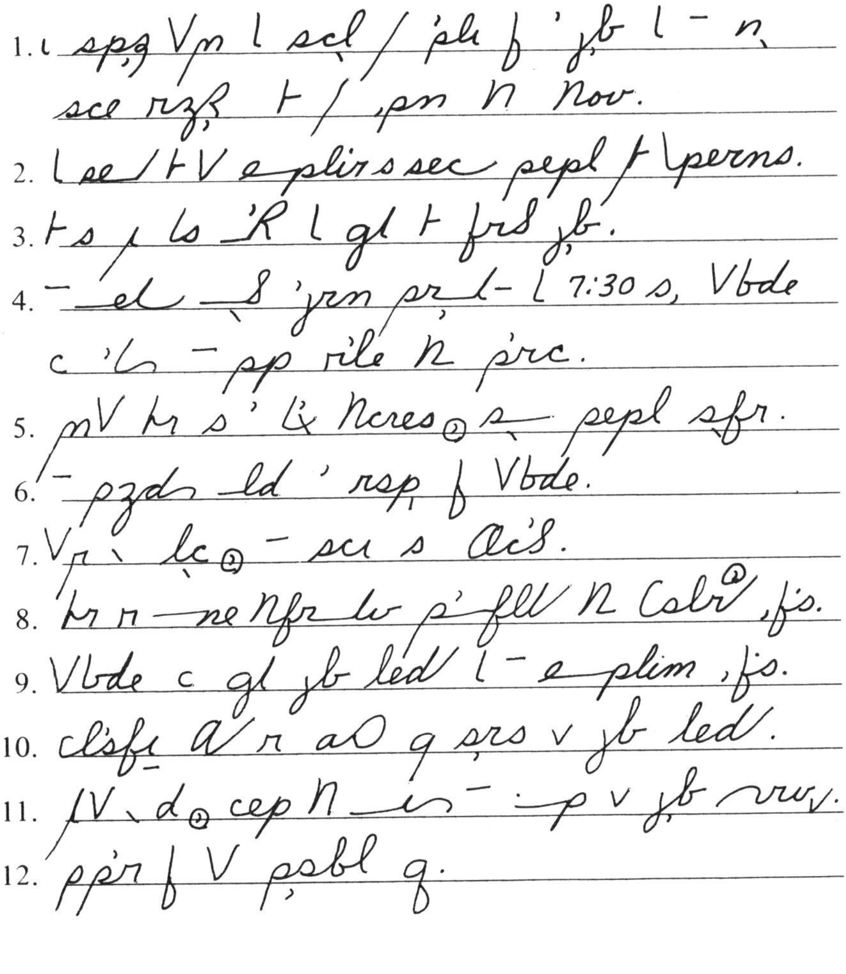

13.
14.
15.

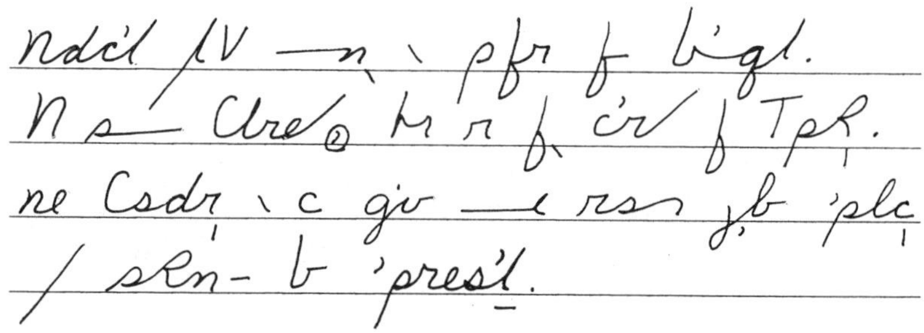

PUNCTUATION REVIEW–ITEMS IN SERIES

Rule for items in series. Use a comma to separate more than 2 words, phrases, or clauses in a series. Most authorities include a comma before *and, nor,* and *or* connecting the last 2 elements in a series.

Examples. The sentences that follow show how commas are used to set off items in series:

1. We took sandwiches, milk, and cake on the picnic.
2. You may find your reference in the dictionary, in the thesaurus, or in the encyclopedia.
3. The sky darkened, the winds blew, and the storm was upon us.
4. The ingredients of music are harmony, tone, rhythm, and orchestration.
5. The detective opened the door, went in, and found the body on the floor.
6. He saw neither the coach, the counselor, nor the principal.

Special caution. You do not use a comma when there are only 2 items. For example, do not insert a comma before *and* and *or* in the following sentences:

1. I will wear a coat and tie to the dance.
2. Are you going to the dance or to the game?

SPELLING PRACTICE

Check the spelling of each of the following words. They are among those most frequently misspelled by college freshmen. After you have studied the spelling of these words, write the outline for each word on a separate piece of paper. Then close your text and write out each word from the outline you have written. Check your spelling with the list in the text and review the words you misspelled.

certain	miniature	relieve
changeable	nickel	repetition
conceive	occurrence	rhythm

NOTETAKING APPLICATIONS

1. Complete the self-checks in Unit 21 in your *Handbook.*
2. Use Tape 5 Side B from the *Notetaking Tape Library* to build speed. If the tapes are not available, your instructor will read the words and sentences to you while you take notes.
3. If time permits, complete the Optional Applications.

KEY TO *NOTES TO READ AND WRITE*

1. The agenda for each board meeting should be sent out at least 14 days before each meeting to assure a quorum. (20)
2. The rules necessary for the fair and efficient conduct of meetings are known as parliamentary procedures. (40)
3. Because unemployment rates are high in some cities, you should make appointments for job interviews well in advance. (60)
4. According to the revised bylaws, one member from each class is to be appointed to the new Student Council. (80)
5. The Student Council proposed that a lounge with soft-drink vending machines be provided in the new facility. (100)
6. The secretary read the minutes of the last meeting, and it was moved and seconded that they be approved as read. (120)
7. The girls and boys were royally entertained by all the employees and really had an enjoyable party. (140)

KEY TO *MORE NOTES TO READ AND WRITE*

1. I suppose everyone at school will apply for a job at the new ski resort that will open in November. (20)
2. It seems that every employer is seeking people with experience.
3. That is why it is hard to get that first job. (40)
4. The meeting must adjourn promptly at 7:30 so everybody can attend the pep rally in the park. (60)
5. Whenever there is a tax increase, some people suffer.
6. The president held a reception for everybody. (80)
7. Everywhere you look, the sky is overcast.
8. There are many informative pamphlets in the counselor's office. (100)
9. Everybody can get job leads at the employment office.
10. Classified ads are another good source of job leads. (120)
11. Whatever you do, keep in mind the importance of job interviews.
12. Prepare for every possible question. (140)
13. Indicate whatever menu you prefer for the banquet.
14. In some countries, there are few cars for transportation. (160)
15. Any consideration you can give my recent job application will certainly be appreciated. (180)

Chapter 22

PLANNING THE JOB SEARCH

Whether or not you plan to go right on with your education, chances are you will be looking for a job in the near future. In this and the following chapter are suggestions for planning and carrying out a job-finding campaign.

JOBS AND THE COLLEGE FRESHMAN

Although jobs are often scarce, most first-year college students manage to find them. For example, a recent survey of college freshmen shows that 2 out of 3 work at least part time.[1]

Students' replies to other financial questions on the survey show that jobs are an integral part of college life. In fact, jobs give first-year college students considerable financial independence. The survey shows that one out of 5 students receives no parental help with college expenses (parents may have helped out with living and other costs, however). One out of 6 (17.4%) was financially independent of parents, and one out of 12 works full time while carrying a full-time academic program.

Obviously, when jobs are so important to college students, there is stiff competition for available positions. All the more reason to concentrate on learning a job skill (typing perhaps) and on gaining some job experience.

PRE-SEARCH PREPARATION

As with most projects you undertake, much of your success on a job search will depend on the quality of your preparation. Here are some suggestions for laying an effective foundation.

Begin the search early. It is common knowledge around most campuses that the choice summer jobs are usually filled before the previous Christmas vacation break. Therefore, to have a reasonable chance of a good summer job, you should have a campaign mapped out by the previous November 1! Similarly, part-time jobs in or near a college town are usually filled long before classes begin in the fall. In fact, many are filled before school closes for the summer term. All the more reason to register with the college placement office as soon as you are admitted. Always try to get the name of a

---

[1] Alexander W. Astin, et al, *The American Freshman: National Norms for Fall 1975* (Los Angeles: Laboratory for Research in Higher Education, University of California, 1976), p. 50.

specific individual so that you will have a personal contact with the placement office. Follow-up phone calls with that individual—even long distance calls—are often very effective reminders of your job needs.

Self-appraisal, a key step. A prospective employer wants to know specifically what you can do and how your skills and abilities fit in with his needs. Therefore, as a first step in merchandising your talents, you should make a realistic inventory of your qualifications and interests. Write down detailed answers to such questions as these:

1. What jobs have I had? Include everything you can think of, even menial tasks.
2. What did I like about each job; What dislikes.
3. What special training have I had? Include such things as typing, sales training, auto mechanics, etc.
4. Do I have special talents or aptitudes? For example, playing a musical instrument, working with children, sports, etc.
5. What are my real interests?
6. What kind of job do I want?

Give serious thought to your answers to the questions above. If you do, you will be able to present your qualifications to the best advantage in job interviews.

Don't depend on your own memory and judgment for your analysis. You may tend to play down your talents and skills or you may overlook an important aspect of your experience. Therefore, try to get a friend or a member of your family to review your analysis.

YOUR PERSONAL DATA SHEET

Perhaps your most important job-hunting tool is your personal data sheet (also known as a resumé). It gives a prospective employer a summary of your job qualifications. In addition to giving personal characteristics, your data sheet should give your educational background, work history, job qualifications, aptitudes, the kinds of jobs you are seeking, and the names and addresses of references (not family members).

Preparation of your data sheet will help you to think methodically about your qualifications, and assembling and organizing the facts about yourself will increase your self-assurance in an interview situation. A suggested form for a data sheet is in "A Writer's Guide to Format" in your *Handbook*.

Obviously, the data sheet should be neatly typed and free from all errors in spelling or fact. If you do not type, have your data sheet typed. Then run off copies as you need them on a copying machine.

Once your data sheet is prepared, you are ready to begin actively searching for a job.

TO CONSIDER AND DISCUSS

1. Explain how another person who knows you may help in developing a self-appraisal for a job hunt.
2. Using the questions in this chapter as a basis, make an inventory of your own qualifications, interests, and aptitudes.

WRITING SHORTCUTS

Combination *electr*. Write a capital E to express the combination *electr* and the following vowel.

Cover the printed words and read the notes until you can read them without hesitating. Write each outline 3 times for speed development. Then write each word only once and try to read your notes back. If there are any words you cannot read, rewrite the outline correctly.

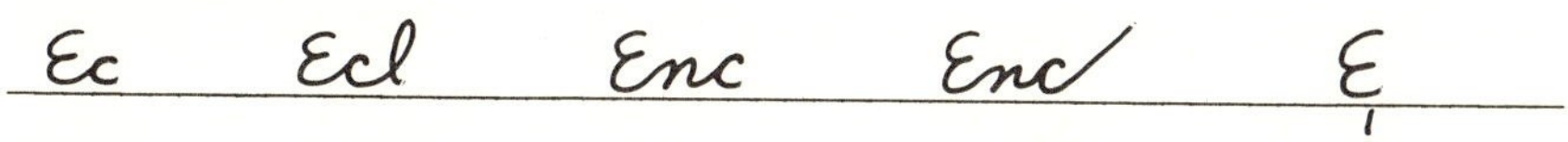

electric **electrical** **electronic** **electronics** **electrician**

electricity **electrification** **electrify** **electron** **electrode**

Combinations *letter-liter*. Write a capital L to express *letter* and *liter.*

As you read each outline, practice writing it several times. Then cover the outlines and write each word once from the print and read back your own notes.

letters **letterhead** **literature** **literary** **newsletter**

Combination *ulate*. Write a small longhand *u* to express the combination *ulate*.

Cover the print and read the words until you can read them without hesitation. Then write each of the outlines 3 times rapidly and accurately.

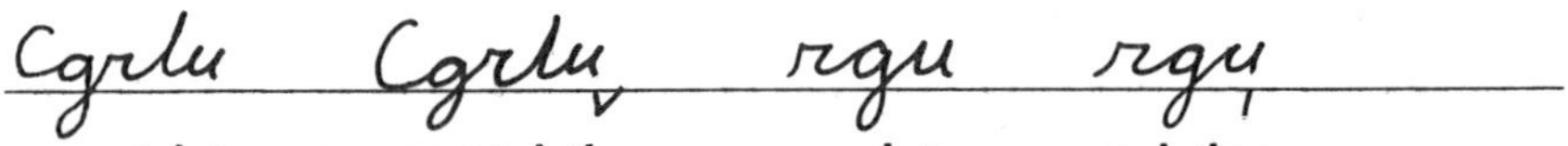

congratulate congratulations regulate regulation

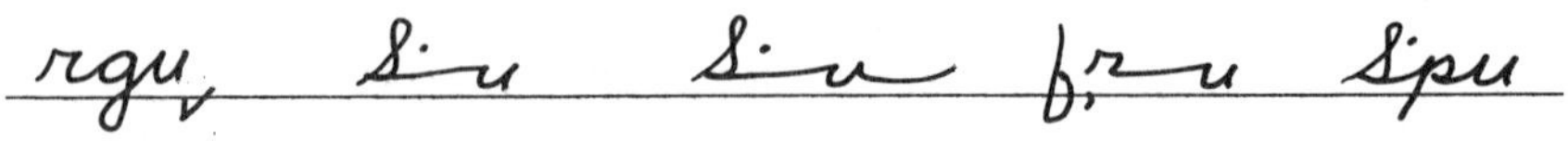

regulations stimulate stimulating formulate stipulate

NOTES TO READ AND WRITE

Read the following notes until you can read them without hesitation. Then turn to the key and write your own notes from the print. Say each sentence to yourself as you write it. Check your notes with those in the text.

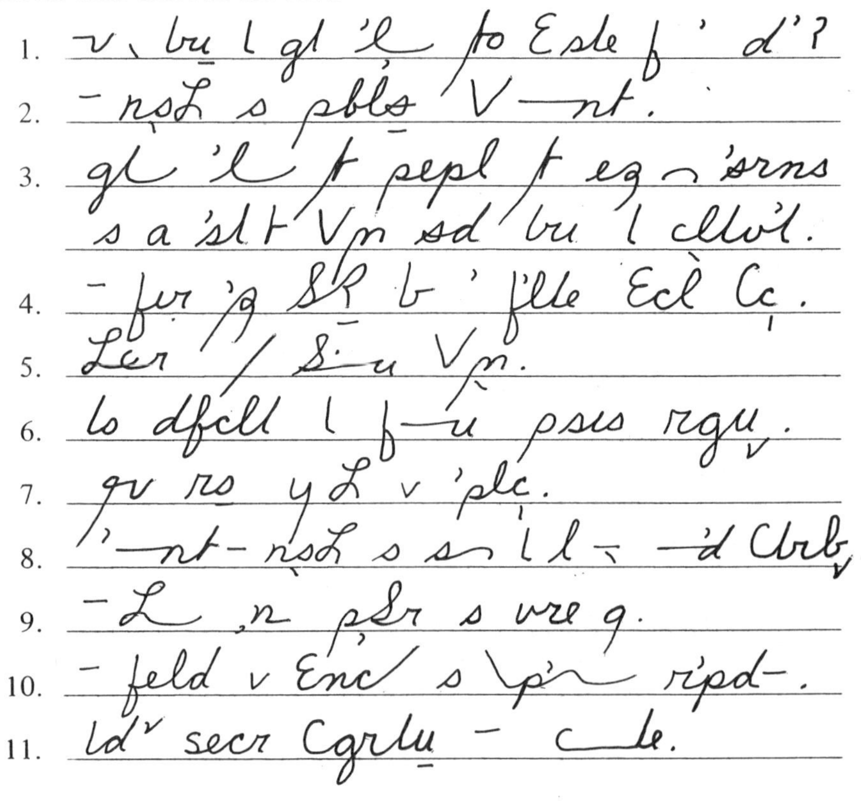

12.

13.

14.

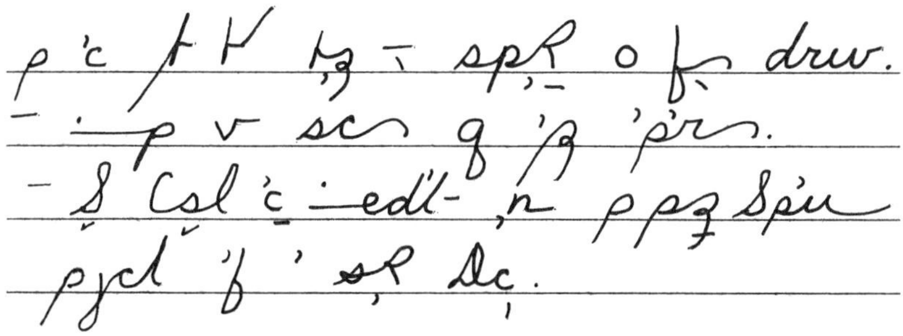

SPELLING PRACTICE

Check the spelling of each of the following words. They are among those most frequently misspelled by college freshmen. After you have studied the spelling of these words, write the outline for each word on a separate piece of paper. Then close your text and write out each word from the outline you have written. Check your spelling with the list in the text and review the words you misspelled.

conscious	omit	seize
decision	opinion	speech
disappear	optimism	strength
disastrous	perform	succeed

PUNCTUATION REVIEW–POSSESSIVES

As you probably know, *possessive* means *belonging to.* Failure to recognize possessives and to form them properly is a frequent error in college students' written work. This review should help you avoid those errors.

Rule for singular possessive. Add an *apostrophe* and an *s* to a singular noun to form the singular possessive.

Examples. Note that each possessive in the sentences below can be restated as "belonging to" or "of."

1. What was the author's point of view? (point of view belonging to one author)
2. I did not understand the professor's homework assignment. (homework assignment of one professor)
3. Joan's sister works after school. (a sister of Joan)

Rule for plural possessives ending in s. Add an *apostrophe* after the *s* to form the possessive of a plural noun ending in *s.*

Examples. Again, note that "belonging to" or "of" can be substituted for the possessive.

1. What was the authors' point of view? (point of view belonging to the authors)
2. The girls' coats were hung in the locker room. (coats belong to the girls)
3. Three days' work was required for the project. (work of 3 days)
4. All of the books' covers were torn off. (covers belonging to the books)

Rule for plural possessives not ending in s. Add an *apostrophe* and an *s* to form the possessive of a plural noun not ending in *s*.

Examples.

1. He wrote children's books. (books belonging to children)
2. The door to the men's lounge was locked. (lounge belonging to men)
3. Women's rights were the subject of the debate. (rights belonging to women)

Special caution. Deciding whether a possessive is plural or singular is sometimes difficult. If in doubt, apply this test: Restate the sentence, substituting *belonging to* or *of* for the possessive. If the resulting noun is plural, you have a plural possessive.

NOTETAKING APPLICATIONS

1. Complete the self-checks in Unit 22 in your *Handbook*.
2. Use Tape 6 Side A from the *Notetaking Tape Library* to build speed. If the tapes are not available, your instructor will read the words and sentences to you while you take notes.
3. If time permits, complete the Optional Applications.

KEY TO *NOTES TO READ AND WRITE*

1. Have you tried to get along without electricity for a day?
2. The newsletter is published every month. (20)
3. Getting along with people with ease and assurance is an asset that everyone should try to cultivate. (40)
4. The fire was started by a faulty electrical connection.
5. Literature will stimulate everyone. (60)

6. It is difficult to formulate precise regulations.
7. We have received your letter of application. (80)
8. A monthly newsletter is sent to all who made contributions.
9. The lettering on the poster is very good. (100)
10. The field of electronics is expanding rapidly.
11. Today's speaker congratulated the committee. (120)
12. Please acknowledge with thanks those who supported our fund drive.
13. The importance of the second question was apparent. (140)
14. The City Council acted immediately on the proposed street-paving project after a short discussion. (160)

Chapter 23

JOB HUNTING

After you have assessed your own capabilities and interests and prepared a personal data sheet, you are ready to seek leads for possible jobs. A thorough search of common sources of job leads can help you to avoid blind alleys that are both discouraging and a waste of time.

SOURCES OF JOBS INFORMATION

From among the many possible sources of jobs, you will need to select those that seem most appropriate to you and to your experience. Here are some sources that are usually worth exploring.

School or college placement office. Once you are admitted to a college, register in the placement office if you want a job. If it is feasible to do so, visit the placement office and faithfully follow up all leads they give you.

Want ads in newspapers. If the college of your choice is in another city, you may want to subscribe briefly to the major newspaper in the area to get an idea of the kinds of jobs that are being advertised. If you find some promising leads, you may want to follow up by telephone or mail.

State employment services. In most states, the local state employment service will list more jobs in more categories than any other single source. Jobs range from highly skilled to unskilled. These services often provide for aptitude and proficiency testing. In many state offices you will be interviewed on your first visit. Thus, you will gain experience in an interview situation.

Telephone book yellow pages. If you have experience in a specialty that is listed in the yellow pages, by all means consult this source for names and addresses of firms in your particular specialty. You should resist the temptation, however, to telephone to ask for a job or to ask, "I was wondering if you have any job openings."

Allies can help. Don't be a lone wolf when it comes to a job search. Use the human resources around you—your friends, relatives, acquaintances, and neighbors. Who knows whom? You do not need high-level contacts within a company to find out specific information—names, possible job openings, etc.—that is so useful in finding a job.

YOUR PROSPECT LIST

As you find job leads from various sources, you should record the essential information about the leads in a uniform manner. Small lined index cards are ideal for this purpose. Prepare one index card for each job possibility. On the card record the following information: name, address, and telephone number of the firm, name of person to contact, date and time of the interview, or other contact. After your first contact, record dates for future contacts and your remarks for future reference.

PLANNING YOUR TIME

Once you begin your search, you should make it a top priority effort, and not an intermittent activity that you engage in when you have nothing else to do.

Search on schedule. Your job hunt will be more successful if you make it a full-time job and devote your full energies to it. If, however, you cannot work at the search full time, then set up a search schedule and stick to it religiously.

Get an early start each day. If you start early, you will have time for several interviews, tests, and other hiring procedures which may be required.

Follow leads immediately. Early editions of papers with want ads can often be purchased at a newspaper office *before* that day's edition is in general circulation. Sometimes an advantage of a few minutes can mean the difference between landing a job and just missing it. If you get a job lead late in the day, don't put off your contact to the next day. Call to make an appointment for the next day.

Be on time. Many good job opportunities have been missed because the applicant was a few minutes late for a job interview. Plan to be a few minutes early for an interview or testing session so you have time to collect your thoughts.

APPLICATION FORMS

Most companies will ask you to fill in an employment application form before they administer tests or arrange for an interview. Your personal data sheet provides answers to most questions on most application blanks. Obviously, application forms should be filled out in ink, so be sure you take a pen with you when applying for a job. Keep in mind that your application is a visual reminder that remains after you have left. Therefore, use extreme care to prepare it carefully and neatly.

THE JOB INTERVIEW

The interview serves 2 purposes. It gives the employer an opportunity to judge your qualifications, appearance, and fitness for the job opening. Equally important, it gives you a chance to consider whether or not the job is one that you want. The interview is an opportunity for you to describe your talents to the best possible advantage. You should not, therefore, take a friend with you to a job interview.

The job interview trips up many job seekers. But it need not cause you difficulty if you rehearse your answers ahead of time so you are prepared to give explicit answers to direct questions.

Prepare for common interview questions. Here is a list of questions that are frequently asked during employment interviews. If you prepare yourself ahead of time to answer each one, you will be able to answer with assurance.

1. In what type of position are you most interested? Why?
2. What jobs have you held? How were they obtained and why did you leave?
3. What are your future vocational plans?
4. In what school activities have you participated? Why? Which did you enjoy the most?
5. How do you spend your spare time? What are your hobbies?
6. Why do you think you might like to work for our company?
7. What qualifications do you have that make you feel you would be successful with our company?
8. Why do you think you would like this particular type of job?
9. What jobs have you enjoyed the most? The least? Why?
10. What school courses did you like best? Least? Why?

Bring essential information. To each interview you should bring at least one copy of your personal data sheet. Be sure that you also have any other information and documents that may be required. For example, you may need proof of your age, a work permit, school records, a driver's license, letters of recommendation from previous employers, and the like.

Ask for suggestions. Not every interview will end up with the question, "When can you come to work?" If there are no job openings at the present time, you can ask "May I keep in touch with you about future possibilities?" Or, you may find that your qualifications are not suitable for the job in question. In such cases, do not hesitate to ask the interviewer to suggest names of other companies that may be interested in your qualifications.

SEEKING INTERVIEWS BY MAIL

Some companies ask for a letter of application as the initial step in the hiring process. Obviously, such letters are extremely important because they are used to select job candidates for further consideration. You may also use a letter of application if you are applying for a job in another city or town.

Letters of application should be typed on good quality white bond paper. Address the letter to a specific individual if you have a name. In such letters, call attention specifically to your experience that relates to the particular job for which you are applying. Enclose a copy of your personal data sheet with your letter.

You will find a sample job-application letter in "A Writer's Guide to Format" in your *Handbook.*

TO CONSIDER AND DISCUSS

1. Draw up a list of all the people you know who might be helpful to you in finding a job.
2. Make a list of jobs for which you feel your experience, training, or interests qualifies you.
3. Using the example in "A Writer's Guide to Format" as a guide, prepare a personal data sheet you could use in seeking a job.

WRITING SHORTCUTS

Combination *bility*. Write a capital  to express the combination *bility*.

Try to read the following notes as fast as you can read the print. Then write each outline and read it back. If any of your notes are difficult to read, rewrite them and read them back. Increase your writing rate by scribble-writing each word several times. Say each word as you write it.

ability **liability** **possibility** **responsibility** **desirability**

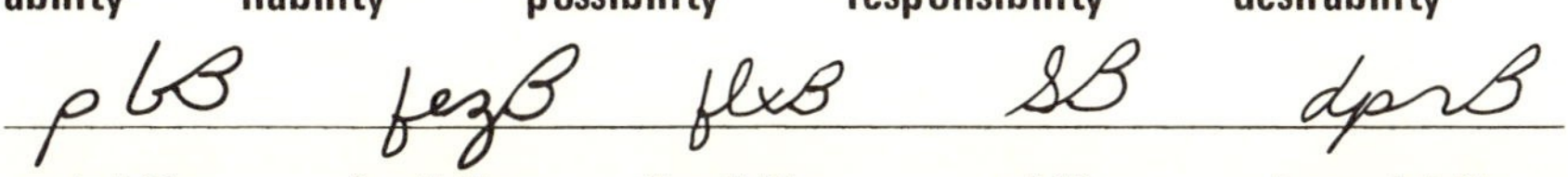

probability **feasibility** **flexibility** **stability** **dependability**

Combination *scribe-script*. Write a printed capital *S* for the combination *scribe-script*.

As you read each word, write its outline 3 times or until you can write it rapidly without any hesitation. Practice reading and writing each word until all are mastered.

describe **inscribe** **description** **subscribe** **transcript**

Suffix *ward*. Write a disjoined *w* symbol to express the suffix *ward*.

As you read each outline, practice writing it until you can do so easily. Say the word each time you write it.

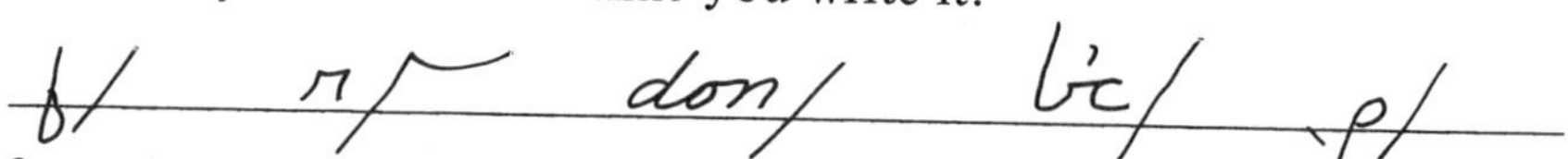

forward **rewarding** **downward** **backward** **upward**

NOTES TO READ AND WRITE

Read the following notes until you can read them without hesitation. Then turn to the key and write your own notes from the print. Say each sentence to yourself as you write it. Check your notes with those in the text.

1\. 2. 3. 4.

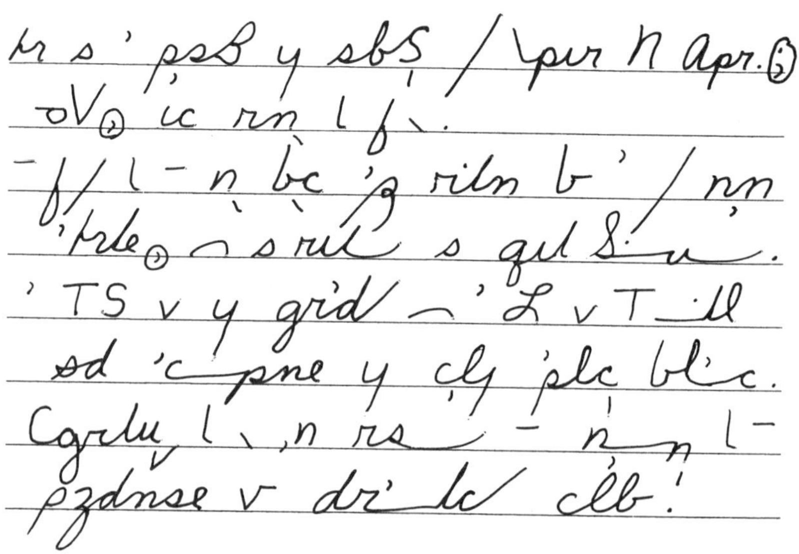

5.
6.
7.
8.
9.

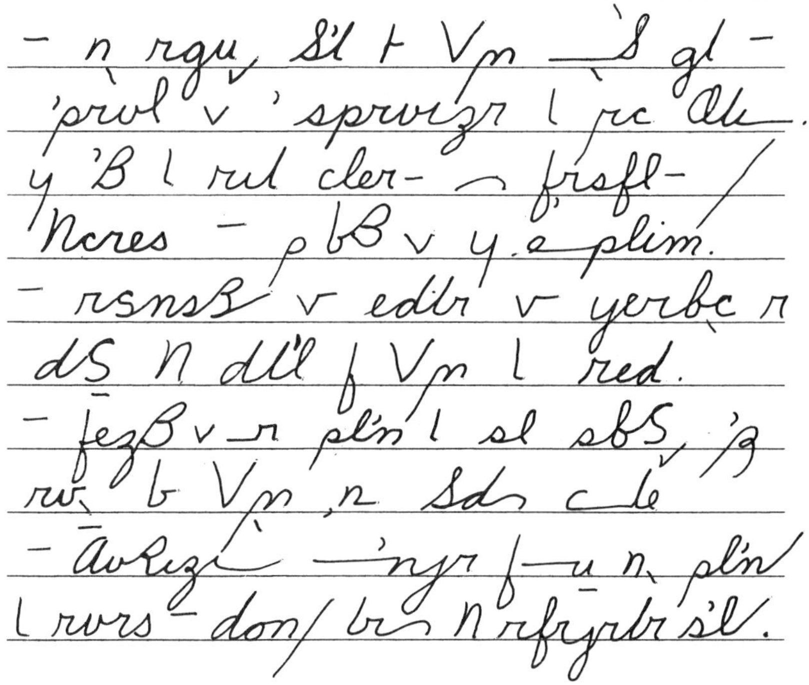

PUNCTUATION REVIEW–INTRODUCTORY CLAUSES

As the name implies, introductory clauses *introduce* the reader to the main part of the sentence. Because introductory clauses give helpful signals to your reader, you should learn to use them in your writing.

Rule for introductory clauses. Introductory clauses should be followed by a comma.

Examples. The sentences that follow include introductory clauses. Note how each clause prepares the reader for the rest of the sentence.

1. Without any warning at all, our instructor assigned a long term paper.
2. Because she doesn't know how to type, Jean paid her roommate to type her paper.
3. Although her roommate is a good typist, Jean found a few errors while proofreading.
4. In order to complete my term paper on time, I found I had to work all weekend.

You should have no difficulty punctuating introductory clauses because they are easy to identify. Many introductory clauses begin with the following words: if, when, as, unless, while, because, although, since, before, after, during, etc.

SPELLING PRACTICE

Check the spelling of each of the following words. They are among those most frequently misspelled by college freshmen. After you have studied the spelling of these words, write the outline for each word on a separate piece of paper. Then close your text and write out each word from the outline you have written. Check your spelling with the list in the text and review the words you misspelled.

divide	pleasant	their
equipped	practical	thorough
excellent	precede	together
existence	prejudice	tragedy

NOTETAKING APPLICATIONS

1. Complete the self-checks in Unit 23 in your *Handbook.*
2. Use Tape 6 Side A from the *Notetaking Tape Library* to build speed. If the tapes are not available, your instructor will read the words and sentences to you while you take notes.
3. If time permits, complete the Optional Applications.

KEY TO *NOTES TO READ AND WRITE*

1. There is a possibility your subscription will expire in April; however, I can renew it for you. (20)
2. The foreword to the new book was written by a well-known authority, and his writing is quite stimulating. (40)
3. A transcript of your grades and a letter of transmittal should accompany your college application blank. (60)
4. Congratulations to you on receiving the nomination to the presidency of the dramatics club. (80)
5. The new regulations state that everyone must get the approval of a supervisor to work overtime. (100)
6. Your ability to write clearly and forcefully will increase the probability of your employment. (120)
7. The responsibilities of the editor of the yearbook are described in detail for everyone to read. (140)
8. The feasibility of her plan to sell subscriptions was reviewed by everyone on the student committee. (160)
9. The advertising manager formulated new plans to reverse the downward trend in refrigerator sales. (160)

Chapter 24

TAKING EXAMINATIONS

Like it or not, tests and examinations are an inescapable fact of life. In one way or another, they have probably already had a bearing on your school career, and you will face many more crucial test situations in your academic career.

But don't think for a moment that you will be free of the pressure of tests once you leave school or college. In fact, the tests you will take out of school will probably be more important in your life than exams facing you in school. In many situations, for example, you will be faced with proficiency examinations when seeking a job. Entrance into many professions is dependent on passing stringent examinations. For example, lawyers, doctors, accountants, and others must demonstrate their knowledge and proficiency before they become full-fledged members of their respective professions.

Because performance on examinations will affect significantly your educational and vocational future, you should resolve now to learn how to take them. With practice and deliberate effort, you can learn to perform better in test situations. If you follow the suggestions that follow, you will learn to display to best advantage the knowledge and skill you bring to every test situation.

PREPARING FOR A TEST

Chances are no one had to remind you to study for your examination for your driver's license. You probably pored over the instructional manual and asked others to drill you on the answers as you counted the days until exam time. When the day of the test finally arrived, you were probably nervous with anticipation. You may have reviewed relevant material before you took the exam, but you didn't cram. Consequently, you didn't panic or get jittery. You were confident that you were well prepared.

To cram or not to cram. Many first-year college students get the idea that cramming must be done if one is to do well on examinations. Actually, however, the effects of intensive cram sessions are invariably unproductive. This kind of self-torture leads to mental and physical exhaustion and can result in panic and confusion at precisely the time when you should be calm and confident.

If you follow the review procedures suggested in this book and keep up reasonably well with your assignments, you should spend the days immediately before an examination in reviewing your reading and lecture notes.

How to review. Obviously, your final review for an examination is important. This is no time for frantically trying to complete the assigned reading. Rather it is a time for pulling together—synthesizing—material from lectures, reading, labs, field trips, and other assignments. Here are some specific suggestions:

1. Focus on the key questions you have turned up in the 2A4R method of study (Chapter 7) and in your "recall" column of your reading and lecture notes (Chapter 9). These key questions will help you direct your attention to the most significant material to be learned.
2. Be particularly attentive during the 3 or 4 class sessions immediately before an examination. During these final class sessions, instructors will often suggest points to review and give other hints that will help you in your review.
3. As you phrase your own review questions, use the key words commonly used in tests. To do this, restate your questions using words such as *evaluate, describe, compare, enumerate.*
4. As you review, practice what you will be required to do in the examination. For example, if you are to take an essay exam, practice organizing and writing answers to essay-type questions. Similarly, if you are to take an objective test, review with objective questions in mind. If you are taking an oral exam, practice organizing and answering "on your feet."
5. Review your performance on previous tests in the course. Concentrate on the types of questions that pulled down your grade. Pay particular attention to the reader's comments on the exam.

The night before. What you do the night before an important examination can determine how well you perform the next day. Plan your evening so you do your final reviewing in a leisurely, uninterrupted fashion. Once you have completed your final reviewing, go to bed. An activity that comes between the time of your final review and the time you will take the test may cause forgetting. A full night's sleep will help you keep alert during the examination.

The day of the exam. Allow plenty of time to take care of all last minute details without rushing around. The pressure of hurrying produces excitement, and the excited person can seldom perform effectively on a test. Some other points to consider are as follows:

1. Collect pens, pencils, paper, etc., needed to take the examination. Bring spares along.
2. Get to the examination room early. If possible, select a seat that will be free of distractions. If you sit near the front, you will usually get your exam questions sooner and you will be less distracted by students arriving late.

3. Try to get into a positive frame of mind. Have confidence—you have prepared well and will do your best.
4. Don't panic. Panic can cause a poor exam score even if you are well prepared. It is self-made and must be self-controlled. If it is not controlled, panic can paralyze one's memory and impair one's ability to write.

TAKING ESSAY TESTS

The essay examination measures your ability to organize your knowledge and to think creatively rather than merely to recall facts you have memorized. To do well on such examinations takes skill in organizing both ideas and time. If you find you often scrawl, "Ran out of time," on the last page of an essay exam, the following suggestions may help:

Read directions carefully. If you are to answer 3 out of 5 questions, don't end up answering 4 or 2.

Read all the questions before you start to write. Then decide how to allocate your time. If you have 3 questions of equal weight to answer and you have 60 minutes, allot 20 minutes to each question. Keep in mind that your first few minutes on a given question will probably be your most productive; therefore, plan to go on to succeeding questions on schedule. If you encounter a question you feel you can't answer, *allocate time for it anyway*.

Plan before you write.To build your confidence, begin with the question that is easiest for you. You will probably save time in the long run and also produce a more coherent answer if you take a few moments to outline your answer or at least to list the points you want to make in your answer. An orderly outline will enable you to write more fluently and eliminate false starts and rewriting.

Get your pen in motion. The first sentence of the first paragraph is often the most difficult part of an answer. Many times you can get started by restating the central part of the question as part of your opening sentence. This approach will also help you to form a direct answer.

Support your ideas. Once you have the first sentence down, support it with facts, ideas, and details. Try to lead your reader from one point to the next in a logical sequence.

Don't save your best for last. Put your most telling points in the first part of your answer. If you don't, you may not be able to work them in at all. Of course, a strong final paragraph is important; but use it to summarize, perhaps again using wording from the original question.

Answer every question. Whether or not you think you know the answer, plan to write something for each question. After you have used your allotted time on the questions you know, turn to those that have caught you by surprise. Seldom will you know absolutely nothing about a question, particularly if you have attended lectures and participated in other class activities. Therefore, start right out with your first sentence, rephrasing the question. Once you get started, you may be surprised at how the ideas begin to flow. You will usually do far better on an exam by *putting something down on every assigned question* rather than by devoting extra time to questions you know.

TAKING OBJECTIVE TESTS

Objective tests—true-false exams, multiple-choice, matching, and completion tests—are used to test a wide range of subject matter and facts in a relatively short period of time. They require recognition of correct responses from among incorrect answers or the ability to recall and provide correct responses. Here are suggestions for improving your performance on these kinds of tests.

Understand the instructions and your options. You should know the answers to these questions:

1. Are you penalized for guessing? If not, you should guess. But if there is a penalty for incorrect answers, you will probably score higher if you answer only those questions you know or feel you may know.
2. Can there be more than one answer to a question?
3. Will the test be machine scored? If so, be sure your answers are recorded properly. Erase completely when you decide to change an answer. Avoid stray pencil marks that might be recorded as an incorrect answer.
4. Do you plan your own time, or is each exam section timed?

Make a quick survey of the exam. If possible, skim the entire exam to see the types of questions and to note the weights assigned to each section.

Read each question with great care. Watch particularly for qualifying words such as *always, most, some, never, usually.* Remember, a preconceived idea can lead you to misread an objective test question. The result: a wrong answer on a subject you know.

Concentrate on your strengths. Many objective tests include more items than can be answered in the time provided. Therefore, you should first answer those items that you know, skipping those you are unsure about. Then, if time permits, go back to tackle those questions you skipped.

Check your paper carefully. If you have time, go back over your answers to be sure you have read the questions properly and answered them accordingly. If you find obvious mistakes, you should correct them. But don't be too quick to change answers. Your first response is likely to be more reliable unless you are sure it is wrong.

TO CONSIDER AND DISCUSS

1. Words commonly used in examination questions have subtle differences in meaning calling for different responses. Using your notetaking skill and a dictionary, jot down definitions for these key words: explain, evaluate, state, relate, illustrate, enumerate, describe, define, compare, and contrast.
2. Be prepared to enumerate ways your approach to taking exams will change as a result of studying this chapter.

NOTES TO READ AND WRITE

Read the following notes until you can read them without hesitation. Then turn to the key and write your own notes from the print. Say each sentence to yourself as you write it. Check your notes with those in the text.

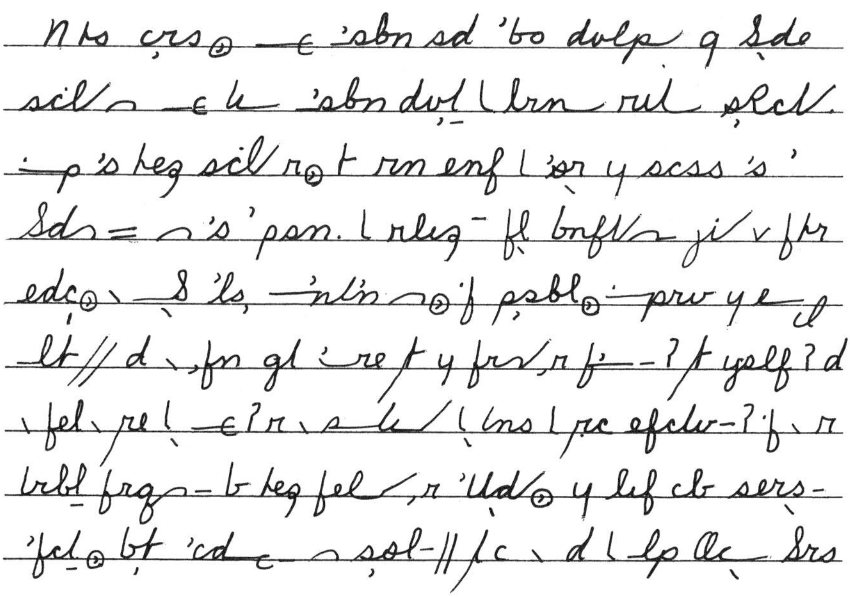

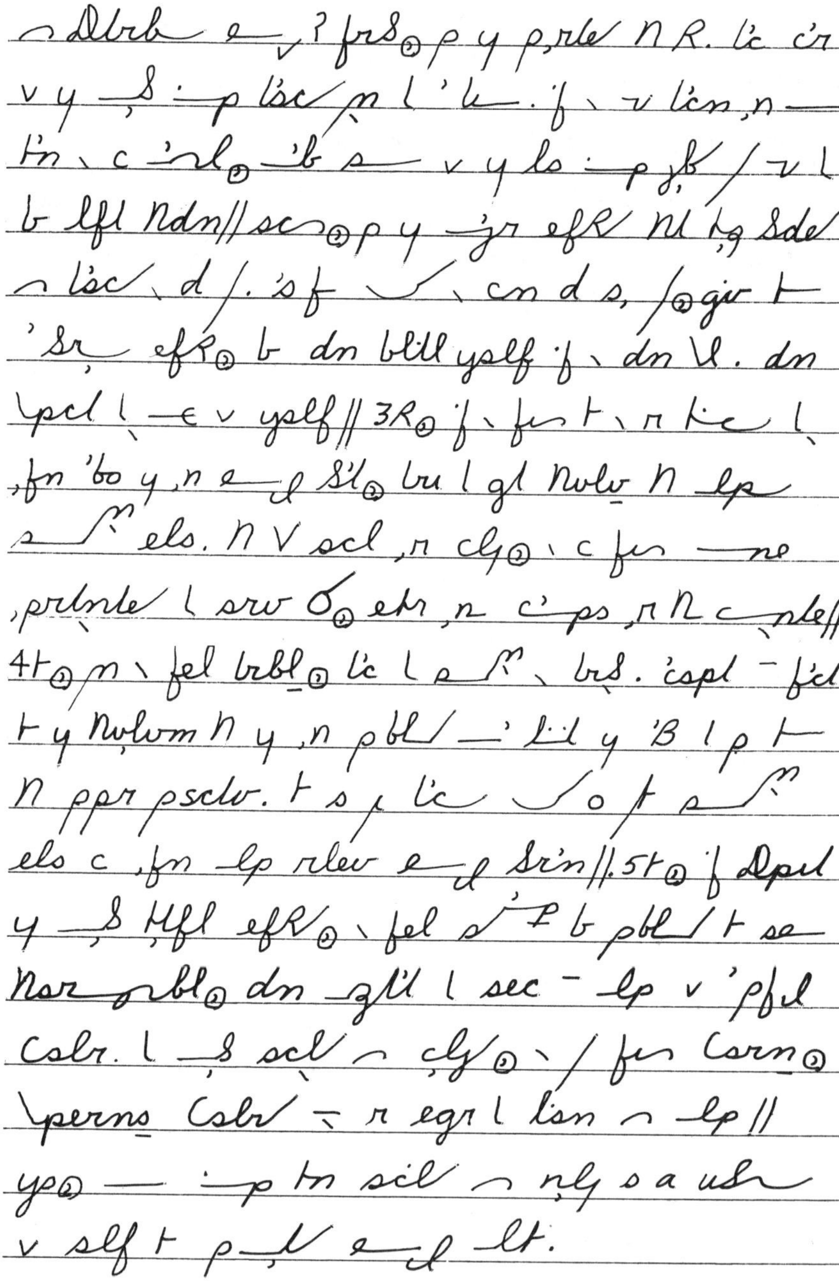

SPELLING PRACTICE

Check the spelling of each of the following words. They are among those most frequently misspelled by college freshmen. After you have studied the spelling of these words, write the outline for each word on a separate piece of paper. Then close your text and write out each word from the outline you have written. Check your spelling with the list in the text and review the words you misspelled.

experience	prevalent	truly
foreign	primitive	usually
grammar	probably	weird
immediately		

CAPITALIZATION REVIEW

Capitals serve 2 major purposes in the English language. They are used to (a) indicate a proper noun or adjective, (b) they signal the beginning of a sentence or sentence fragment. Because there are many rules governing capitalization, it is wise to consult a dictionary when in doubt. You will find additional rules for capitalization in "A Writer's Guide to Style" in your *Handbook.*

1. Canada and the United States have been good neighbors for a long time. (names of countries)
2. Dr. Gerald Frye and Professor Fred Smith are outstanding researchers. (titles and names of people)
3. Read *The Wall Street Journal* for the latest stock market report. (names of newspapers, books, etc.)
4. Does Easter fall on Sunday, April 15, this year? (days, months, holidays)
5. We learned a few Danish words before we went to Denmark and other Scandanavian countries. (languages, countries, geographic areas)

KEY TO *NOTES TO READ AND WRITE*

In this course, much has been said about developing good study skills and much time has been devoted to learning (20) writing shortcuts. Important as these skills are, they are not enough to assure your success as a student—and as (40) a person. To realize the full benefits and the joys of further education, you must also maintain (60) and, if possible, improve your emotional health.

Do you often get angry with your friends or family? With (80) yourself? Do you feel you worry too much? Are you sometimes too tense to work effectively? If you are troubled frequently (100) by these feelings or attitudes, your life can be seriously affected, both academically and (120) socially.

What can you do to help overcome stress and disturbing emotions? First, put your priorities in (140) order. Take care of your most important tasks one at a time. If you have taken on more than you can handle, maybe (160) some of your less important jobs will have to be left undone.

Second, put your major efforts into those studies (180) and tasks you do well. As for the things you cannot do so well, give them a strong effort, but do not belittle yourself (200) if you do not excel. Do not expect too much of yourself.

Third, if you find that you are thinking too often (220) about your own emotional state, try to get involved in helping someone else. In every school or college, (240) you can find many opportunities to serve others, either on the campus or in the community.

Fourth, (260) when you feel troubled, talk to someone you trust. Accept the fact that your involvement in your own problems may limit (280) your ability to put them in proper perspective. That is why talking things out with someone else can often (300) help relieve emotional strain.

Fifth, if despite your most thoughtful efforts, you feel swamped by problems that seem insurmountable, (320) do not hesitate to seek the help of a professional counselor. At most schools and colleges, (340) you will find concerned, experienced counselors who are eager to listen and help.

Yes, more important than skills (360) and knowledge is an understanding of self that promotes emotional health. (377)

NOTETAKING APPLICATIONS

1. Complete the self-checks in Unit 24 in your *Handbook.*
2. Use Tape 6 Side B from the *Notetaking Tape Library* to build speed. If the tapes are not available, your instructor will read the words and sentences to you while you take notes.
3. If time permits, complete the Optional Applications.

FINAL EXAMINATION

When directed to do so by your instructor, remove and take the Final Examination that is bound in the back of your *Handbook*. This test covers the material that has been presented in the 24 chapters of your textbook.

List of Spelling Words

Index of Writing Shortcuts

General Index

SPELLING WORDS

The following words are reviewed in various chapters in this text. The list is adapted from: Edna L. Furness and Gertrude A. Boyd, "Real Spelling Demons for College Students," *College English,* March 1970, pp. 292-295.

absence
accidentally
accommodate
across
advise
all right
almost
already
among
analysis
analyze
apparent
appearance
arguing
argument
beginning
believe
benefit
benefited
business
certain
changeable
choose
coming
committee
conceive
conscientious
conscious
controlled
decision
definite
despair
develop
disappoint
disappear
disastrous
disease
divide
divine
effect
equipped
embarrass
environment
excellent
existence
experience
familiar
fascinate
February
finally
foreign
friend
generally
government
governor
grammar
heroes
immediately
incidentally
intelligence

irrelevant
its
judgment
knowledge
laboratory
laid
led
library
loneliness
lose
maintenance
marriage
mathematics
meant
medicine
miniature
morale
necessary
nickel
noticeable
occurrence
occurred
omit

opinion
optimism
parallel
perform
pleasant
practical
precede
prejudice
prevalent
primitive
privilege
probably
procedure
proceed
professor
pursue
pursuit
quantity
receive
recommend
relieve
repetition
rhythm

safety
schedule
seize
separate
shining
similar
speech
strength
studying
succeed
their
there
thorough
together
tragedy
truly
until
usually
villain
weather
weird
whether
whose
writing

INDEX AND SUMMARY OF WRITING SHORTCUTS

SOUNDS OR COMBINATIONS	EXPRESSED BY		ILLUSTRATIONS	PAGE
a	'		aid 'd tall t'l	9
ad (p)	a		adverse avrs	40
an (p)	a		answer asr	52
ax-ex-ox (p)	\		axis \s	105
be (p)	b		belief blef	26
bility	↗B		ability 'B	133
c (hard)-k	c		cake c'c	6
c (soft)	s		race r's	5
ch	ϲ̶		chase ϲ̶'s	34
con-coun	C		convict Cvic	26
d (past tense)	—		noted nt̲	48
de (p)	d		delay dl'	26
des-dis	D or D		despair Dp'r	53
e (long)	e		feel fel	5
e (short)			fell fl	9
ed (past tense)	_		tried tri̲	48
electr	Ē		electric Ēc	125
en-in-un (p)	N		envy Nve	40
ever-every	V	(d)	everybody Vbde	118
ex (p)	\		exist \s	105
extr	x		extreme x—	105
for-fore-fur (p)	f	(d)	forgive fgiv	73
g (soft)	j		large l'j	5
h	–		had –'d	33
i (long)	ι		night nit	5
i (short)	·		bill b·l	10
in (p)	N		insight Nsit	40
ing-ng	‿		ringing r·‿‿	56
j	j	(no dot)	jail j'l	5
k	c		kick c·c	6
letter-liter	L		literary L're	125
ly (s)	–	(d)	likely lic-	56

(p) = prefix; (s) = suffix; (d) = disjoined

SOUNDS OR COMBINATIONS	EXPRESSED BY		ILLUSTRATIONS	PAGE
m	—		meter —elr	14
ment	m		basement b'sm	15
nd-nt	⌒		find fn	61
o	,		slow sl, cot c,l	10
oi-oy	i	(dotted)	soil sil	98
oo	\		room r—	14
other	O		another aO	111
ou-ow-out	o		stout Sod	87
over	O		overtake Ol'c	111
ox (p)	\		oxide \id	105
per-pre-pri-pro-pur	p	(d)	person psn	73
qu	q		quick qic	79
rd-rt	R		accord 'cR	79
re (p)	r		reply rpl	26
s (added to word)	/		trees tre/ days d/	15
s (hard)	z		reason rzn	5
s (soft)	s		see se	5
scribe-script	S		inscribe NS	134
sh	s		she se	33
sion-tion	,	(d)	tension tn,	26
sp	s		speak sec	62
st	S		steel Sel	40
t	l		time tu—	5
th	t		them t—	33
thing	⌣		nothing n⌣	56
tion	,		nation n,	26
trans	T	(d)	translate Tl'l	111
u			duty dte up p	14
ulate	u		formulate f—u	126
un (p)	n		unfair nf'r	40
under	u		undertake ul'c	80
w-wh	/		work rc when n	52
ward	/	(d)	forward f/	134

GENERAL INDEX